Sweet TREATS

A collection of miniature cakes, pastries, biscuits, slices and macaroons

Published in 2010 by ACP Books, Sydney
ACP Books are published by
ACP Magazines a division of
PBL Media Pty Limited

acp books

ACP BOOKS

General manager Christine Whiston
Associate publisher Seymour Cohen
Editor-in-chief Susan Tomnay
Creative director & designer
Hieu Chi Nguyen
Senior editor Stephanie Kistner
Food director Pamela Clark
Sales & rights director Brian Cearnes
Marketing manager Bridget Cody
Senior business analyst Rebecca Varela
Operations manager David Scotto
Production manager Victoria Jefferys

Published by ACP Books,
a division of ACP Magazines Ltd.
54 Park St, Sydney NSW Australia 2000.
GPO Box 4088, Sydney, NSW 2001.
Phone +61 2 9282 8618
Fax +61 2 9267 9438
acpbooks@acpmagazines.com.au
www.acpbooks.com.au

To order books,
phone 136 116 (within Australia) or
order online at www.acpbooks.com.au

Send recipe enquiries to:
recipeenquiries@acpmagazines.com.au

Printed by Toppan Leefung Printing Limited, China.

Australia Distributed by Network Services, GPO Box 4088, Sydney, NSW 2001.
Phone +61 2 9282 8777 Fax +61 2 9264 3278
networkweb@networkservicescompany.com.au
New Zealand Distributed by Southern Publishers Group, 21 Newton Rd, Auckland.
Phone +64 9 360 0692 Fax +64 9 360 0695 hub@spg.co.nz
South Africa Distributed by PSD Promotions, 30 Diesel Road Isando, Gauteng
Johannesburg. PO Box 1175, Isando 1600, Gauteng Johannesburg.
Phone +27 11 392 6065/6/7 Fax +27 11 392 6079/80 orders@psdprom.co.za

Title: Sweet treats / compiler, Pamela Clark.
ISBN 978-1-86396-868-3
Notes: Includes index.
Subjects: Desserts. Cakes.
Other authors/contributors: Clark, Pamela
Dewey number: 641.86

Originally published in two editions: *Sweet* in 2007 and *Chocolate* in 2008.

Photographers Joshua Dasey, Louise Lister, John Paul Urizar
Stylists Margot Braddon, Vicki Liley
Food styling & preparation Angela Muscat, Rebecca Squadrito, Nicole Dicker

Cover Chocolate éclairs, page 25
Cover photographer Louise Lister
Cover stylist Vicki Liley
Back cover Raspberry rapture ice-cream cakes, page 117
Back cover photographer John Paul Urizar
Back cover stylist Margot Braddon

The publishers would like to thank the following for props used in photography
Tres Fabu; No Chintz; Roylston House Fabrics; Pigotts Store; The Essential Ingredient;
Westbury Textiles; Kikki K; Vitra (Unifor); Space Furniture; Imagine This; le bonbon;
Gin & Tonic; Dedece; Macleay on Manning; Mokum; Radford Furnishings; Third Drawer
Down; Top3 by Design.

THE AUSTRALIAN
Women's Weekly

Sweet TREATS

A collection of miniature cakes, pastries, biscuits, slices and macaroons

acp books

contents

Treat yourself to something special. In this book you'll find a treasure trove of recipes -- all sorts of luscious desserts, cakes, slices, biscuits, preserves, petits fours, sweet dainty bite-sized morsels, truffles, and, some truly unique goodies to make for gifts. Chocolate is the star – rich, creamy, dark, white and milk – they're all here – and, we've combined chocolate with caramel, coffee, liqueurs and too many other flavours to mention.

Pamela Clark

Food Director

chocolate treats

Ever since the Aztecs first tasted the fruit of the
cocoa tree, we haven't been able to resist chocolate.
Its smooth sensual taste seduces the taste buds in
rich cakes, creamy desserts, chewy brownies and
sumptuous tea-time treats. The divine recipes in
this chapter range from the decadent to the delicate.

chocolate crowned sticky date cakes

120g (4 ounces) dark eating
(semi-sweet) chocolate, melted
1¾ cups (250g) seeded
dried dates
1 teaspoon bicarbonate of
(baking) soda
1 cup (250ml) boiling water
60g (2 ounces) butter, chopped
¾ cup (165g) firmly packed
light brown sugar
2 eggs
1 cup (150g) self-raising flour
80g (2½ ounces) dark eating
(semi-sweet) chocolate,
chopped coarsely

chocolate butterscotch sauce
½ cup (110g) firmly packed
light brown sugar
⅔ cup (160ml) pouring cream
50g (1½ ounces) butter
1 tablespoon cocoa powder,
sifted

1 Preheat oven to 180°C/350°F.
Grease 6-hole (¾ cup/180ml)
texas muffin pan; line bases with
baking paper.
2 Spread melted chocolate
over base of each pan hole;
refrigerate until set.
3 Meanwhile, combine dates,
soda and the water in food
processor, put lid in position;
stand 5 minutes. Process until
smooth. Add butter and sugar;
process until combined. Add eggs
and flour; pulse until combined.
Stir in chopped chocolate.
4 Divide mixture among pan
holes; bake about 15 minutes.
Stand cakes 2 minutes; turn
onto wire rack to cool slightly.
Remove paper.
5 Make chocolate butterscotch
sauce.
6 Serve warm cakes drizzled
with sauce and topped with
whipped cream, if you like.
chocolate butterscotch sauce
Stir ingredients in medium
saucepan over heat, without
boiling, until sugar dissolves; bring
to the boil. Remove from heat.

makes 6

ginger chocolate creams

125g (4 ounces) unsalted
   butter, softened
⅓ cup (75g) firmly packed
   light brown sugar
2 tablespoons golden syrup
½ cup (75g) self-raising flour
⅔ cup (100g) wholemeal
   self-raising flour
1 teaspoon ground ginger
1 tablespoon cocoa powder
chocolate ginger cream
¼ cup (60ml) pouring cream
150g (5 ounces) milk eating
   chocolate, chopped coarsely
¼ cup (55g) finely chopped
   glacé ginger

1 Beat butter and sugar in small bowl with electric mixer until light and fluffy. Beat in golden syrup. Stir in sifted dry ingredients, in two batches. Knead on floured surface until smooth.
2 Roll dough between sheets of baking paper until 5mm (¼-inch) thick; refrigerate 30 minutes.
3 Meanwhile, make chocolate ginger cream.
4 Preheat oven to 180°C/350°F. Grease two oven trays; line with baking paper.
5 Cut 32 x 5.5cm (2¼-inch) rounds from dough; place on trays.
6 Bake biscuits about 5 minutes; cool on trays. Sandwich biscuits with chocolate ginger cream.
chocolate ginger cream Stir cream and chocolate in small heatproof bowl over small saucepan of simmering water until smooth. Stir in ginger; refrigerate until spreadable.

makes 16

cardamom orange mousse cakes

You can use a 300ml carton of cream in this recipe.

50g (1½ ounces) dark eating (semi-sweet) chocolate, melted
25g (¾ ounce) unsalted butter, melted
125g (4 ounces) butternut snap biscuits
25g (¾ ounce) unsalted butter, melted, extra
1 teaspoon finely grated orange rind
¼ teaspoon ground cardamom

orange mousse
1¼ cup (310ml) thickened (heavy) cream
150g (4½ ounces) dark eating (semi-sweet) chocolate, chopped coarsely
1 teaspoon finely grated orange rind
¼ teaspoon ground cardamom

orange syrup
⅔ cup (160ml) orange juice
¼ cup (55g) caster (superfine) sugar
2 tablespoons finely shredded orange rind

1 Make orange mousse.
2 Grease 12-hole (¼ cup/60ml) mini cheesecake pan with removable bases; line bases with baking paper.
3 Combine chocolate and butter, spoon into holes; cool 5 minutes.
4 Process biscuits until fine. Add extra butter, rind and cardamom; process until combined. Divide mixture among pan holes; press firmly over chocolate bases.
5 Divide mousse among pan holes; refrigerate overnight.
6 Make orange syrup.
7 Serve mousse cakes with orange syrup.

orange mousse Stir ingredients in small heatproof bowl over small saucepan of simmering water until smooth. Refrigerate about 30 minutes or until cool. Beat mousse mixture with electric mixer for 2 minutes or until mixture changes to a paler colour. Do not overbeat or mixture will curdle.
orange syrup Stir juice and sugar in small saucepan, over heat, without boiling, until sugar dissolves. Add rind; bring to the boil. Reduce heat; simmer, uncovered, about 10 minutes or until syrup thickens slightly. Cool.

makes 12

chocolate shortbread stars

250g (8 ounces) unsalted
   butter, softened
1 cup (160g) icing
   (confectioners') sugar
1¼ cups (185g) plain
   (all-purpose) flour
½ cup (100g) rice flour
¼ cup (25g) cocoa powder
150 dark Choc Bits (60g)
2 tablespoons icing
   (confectioners') sugar, extra

1 Beat butter and sugar in medium bowl with electric mixer until light and fluffy. Stir in sifted flours and cocoa, in two batches. Knead on floured surface until smooth. Roll dough between sheets of baking paper until 1cm (½-inch) thick; refrigerate 30 minutes.
2 Preheat oven to 160°C/325°F fan-forced. Grease two oven trays; line with baking paper.
3 Cut 25 x 6.5cm (2¾-inch) stars from dough. Place stars about 4cm (1½ inches) apart on trays. Decorate with Choc Bits.
4 Bake stars about 20 minutes; cool on trays. Dust stars with extra sifted icing sugar.

makes 25

185g (6 ounces) unsalted
    butter, softened
¾ cup (165g) firmly packed
    light brown sugar
1¼ cups (185g) plain
    (all-purpose) flour
⅓ cup (65g) finely chopped
    dried figs
½ cup (60g) finely chopped
    roasted pecans
½ cup (95g) dark Choc Bits
100g (3 ounces) dark eating
    (semi-sweet) chocolate,
    melted

1 Preheat oven to 180°C/350°F
fan-forced. Grease 20cm x 30cm
(8-inch x 12-inch) lamington pan;
line base with baking paper,
extending paper 5cm (2 inches)
over long sides.
2 Beat butter and sugar in small
bowl with electric mixer until
light and fluffy. Stir in sifted flour,
then figs, nuts and Choc Bits.
Press mixture into pan.
3 Bake slice about 25 minutes.
Mark slice into 24 squares.
Cool slice in pan; drizzle with
chocolate. Cut into squares
when chocolate is set.

makes 24

choc-chip, fig and pecan slice

pom poms

395g (12½ ounces) canned
  sweetened condensed milk
30g (1 ounce) unsalted butter
1 cup (140g) finely chopped
  roasted unsalted peanuts
4 cups (40g) air-popped popcorn
½ cup (40g) toasted shredded
  coconut
200g (6½ ounces) milk eating
  chocolate, melted

1 Line two trays with baking paper.
2 Combine condensed milk and butter in large heavy-based saucepan; cook, stirring, over medium heat, about 10 minutes or until mixture is a caramel colour. Remove from heat; quickly stir in nuts, popcorn and coconut.
3 Working quickly, roll walnut-sized pieces of mixture into balls. Dip balls in chocolate; place on trays. Refrigerate until firm.

makes 40

chocolate hazelnut thins

1 egg white
¼ cup (55g) light brown sugar
2 tablespoons plain
   (all-purpose) flour
2 teaspoons cocoa powder
30g (1 ounce) butter, melted
1 teaspoon milk
1 tablespoon ground hazelnuts

1 Preheat oven to 180°C/350°F. Grease oven trays.
2 Beat egg white in small bowl with electric mixer until soft peaks form; gradually add sugar, beating until sugar dissolves. Stir in sifted flour and cocoa, then butter, milk and ground hazelnuts.
3 Spread level teaspoons of mixture into 8cm (3¼-inch) circles, about 4cm (1½ inches) apart on trays.
4 Bake thins, in batches, about 5 minutes. Remove from tray immediately using metal spatula, place over rolling pin to cool (see page 243).

makes 24

chocolate éclairs

15g (½ ounce) butter
¼ cup (60ml) water
¼ cup (35g) plain
  (all-purpose) flour
1 egg

custard cream
1 vanilla bean
1 cup (250ml) milk
3 egg yolks
⅓ cup (75g) caster
  (superfine) sugar
2 tablespoons pure cornflour
  (cornstarch)
⅓ cup (80ml) thickened (heavy)
  cream, whipped

chocolate glaze
30g (1 ounce) dark eating
  (semi-sweet) chocolate,
  chopped coarsely
30g (1 ounce) milk eating
  chocolate, chopped coarsely
15g (½ ounce) butter

1 Make custard cream.
2 Preheat oven to 220°C/425°F. Grease two oven trays.
3 Bring butter and the water to the boil in small saucepan. Add flour, beat with wooden spoon over heat until mixture comes away from base and side of pan and forms a smooth ball (see page 243).
4 Transfer mixture to small bowl; beat in egg with electric mixer until mixture becomes glossy (see page 243). Spoon pastry mixture into piping bag fitted with 1cm (½-inch) plain tube. Pipe 5cm (2-inch) lengths about 5cm (2 inches) apart on trays; bake 7 minutes.
5 Reduce oven to 180°C/350°F; bake éclairs further 10 minutes. Using serrated knife, cut éclairs in half, remove any soft centres; return to trays, bake 5 minutes or until dry to touch. Cool on trays.
6 Make chocolate glaze.
7 Spoon custard cream into piping bag fitted with 5mm (¼-inch) fluted tube. Pipe custard cream into 16 pastry bases, top with pastry tops. Spread with chocolate glaze.

custard cream Split vanilla bean, scrape seeds into milk in small saucepan (discard bean); bring to the boil. Meanwhile, beat egg yolks, sugar and cornflour in small bowl with electric mixer until thick. With motor operating, gradually beat in hot milk mixture. Return custard to pan; stir over heat until mixture boils and thickens. Cover surface of custard with plastic wrap, refrigerate 1 hour. Fold cream into custard, in two batches.

chocolate glaze Stir ingredients in small heatproof bowl over small saucepan of simmering water until smooth. Use while warm.

makes 16

chocolate, apricot and hazelnut cake

1⅔ cups (250g) dried apricots, chopped finely
½ cup (125ml) water
250g (8 ounces) butter, softened
2 cups (440g) firmly packed light brown sugar
6 eggs
1 cup (150g) plain (all-purpose) flour
½ cup (75g) self-raising flour
¼ cup (25g) cocoa powder
1 cup (110g) ground hazelnuts
⅔ cup (160ml) buttermilk

chocolate buttermilk cream
300g (9½ ounces) milk eating chocolate, chopped coarsely
½ cup (125ml) buttermilk
1 cup (160g) icing (confectioners') sugar

1 Combine apricots and the water in small saucepan; bring to the boil. Reduce heat; simmer, covered, stirring occasionally, about 10 minutes or until apricots are soft. Cool.

2 Preheat oven to 180°C/350°F. Grease deep 22cm (8¾-inch) round cake pan; line with baking paper.

3 Beat butter and sugar in small bowl with electric mixer until light and fluffy. Beat in eggs, one at a time. Transfer mixture to large bowl; stir in apricot mixture, sifted flours and cocoa, ground hazelnuts and buttermilk, in two batches.

4 Spread mixture into pan; bake about 1 hour 50 minutes. Stand cake 10 minutes; turn, top-side up, onto wire rack to cool.

5 Meanwhile, make chocolate buttermilk cream.

6 Split cold cake into three layers; sandwich layers with two-thirds of the buttermilk cream. Spread cake with remaining buttermilk cream. Top with dark chocolate curls (see page 230), if you like.

chocolate buttermilk cream
Stir chocolate and buttermilk in small heatproof bowl over small saucepan of simmering water until smooth; stir in sifted icing sugar. Refrigerate, stirring occasionally, about 30 minutes, or until spreadable.

serves 12

You will need 36 foil petit four cases for this recipe.

1 cup (150g) frozen raspberries, thawed
¼ cup (60ml) pouring cream
2 tablespoons raspberry-flavoured liqueur
200g (6½ ounces) milk eating chocolate, chopped coarsely
36 frozen raspberries, extra

1 Push raspberries through a fine sieve into small heatproof bowl; discard seeds.
2 Add cream, liqueur and chocolate to bowl; stir over small saucepan of simmering water until smooth.
3 Divide half the chocolate mixture among cases; top with extra raspberries. Top with remaining chocolate mixture. Freeze truffles until firm.
4 Remove truffles from freezer 5 minutes before serving. Serve topped with edible gold leaf, if you like.

makes 36

frozen raspberry truffles

150g (4½ ounces) dark eating
  (semi-sweet) chocolate,
  chopped coarsely
⅓ cup (80ml) pouring cream
40g (1½ ounces) unsalted butter
100g (3 ounces) quince paste
¼ cup (35g) coarsely chopped
  roasted hazelnuts
pastry
¾ cup (110g) plain
  (all-purpose) flour
¼ cup (25g) cocoa powder
¼ cup (40g) icing
  (confectioners') sugar
90g (3 ounces) cold unsalted
  butter, chopped
1 egg yolk
1 tablespoon iced water,
  approximately

1 Make pastry.
2 Grease two 12-hole
(1½-tablespoon/30ml) shallow
round-based patty pans with
butter. Roll rounded teaspoons
of pastry into balls, press over
base and side of holes. Prick
pastry all over with fork.
Refrigerate 30 minutes.
3 Preheat oven to 180°C/350°F.
4 Bake pastry cases 10 minutes.
5 Meanwhile, stir chocolate,
cream and butter in small
heatproof bowl over small
saucepan of simmering water
until smooth. Cool 15 minutes.

6 Soften paste in microwave
oven on MEDIUM (75%) for
about 20 seconds.
7 Divide paste among pastry
cases; top with half of the nuts.
Top with chocolate mixture, then
remaining nuts. Refrigerate 1 hour.
pastry Process sifted flour,
cocoa, icing sugar and butter
until crumbly. Add egg yolk
and enough of the water
until ingredients just come
together when processed.
Knead dough on floured surface
until smooth. Enclose in plastic
wrap; refrigerate 30 minutes.

makes 24

chocolate, quince and hazelnut tartlets

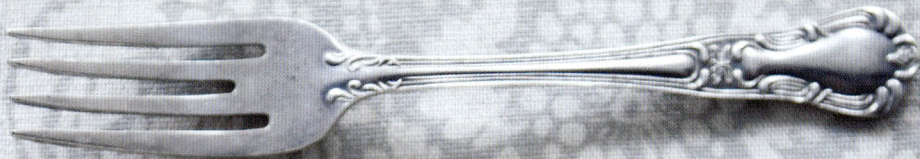

warm malt truffle muffins

1¼ cups (185g) self-raising flour
¼ cup (30g) malted milk powder
2 tablespoons cocoa powder
pinch bicarbonate of
   (baking) soda
¼ cup (55g) light brown sugar
60g (2 ounces) unsalted butter
⅓ cup (125g) barley malt syrup
½ cup (125ml) milk
1 egg
¾ cup (180ml) pouring cream
malt truffles

200g (6½ ounces) milk eating
   chocolate, chopped coarsely
¼ cup (60ml) pouring cream
½ cup (60g) malted milk powder

1 Make malt truffles.
2 Preheat oven to 180°C/350°F.
Line 12-hole (⅓ cup/80ml) muffin
pan with paper cases.
3 Sift flour, malt powder, cocoa,
soda and sugar into medium bowl.
4 Stir butter and malt syrup in
small saucepan over low heat
until smooth.
5 Stir butter mixture, milk and egg
into flour mixture. Do not over-mix;
mixture should be lumpy. Divide
half the mixture among cases.
Place a truffle into each case;
top with remaining mixture.
6 Bake muffins about 20 minutes;
cool 2 minutes, then remove
paper cases.
7 Meanwhile, stir reserved malt
truffle mixture and cream in
small saucepan, over low heat,
until malt sauce is smooth.
8 Serve warm muffins with
warm sauce. Dust with sifted
cocoa powder, if you like.

malt truffles Stir ingredients in
small heatproof bowl over small
saucepan of simmering water
until smooth. Reserve ½ cup
(125ml) mixture for malt sauce.
Refrigerate remaining mixture
about 30 minutes or until firm.
Roll heaped teaspoons of
refrigerated mixture into balls;
place on baking-paper-lined tray.
Freeze until firm.

makes 12

33

2 cups (500ml) water

2 cups (440g) caster
   (superfine) sugar

4 x 5cm (2-inch) strips
   orange rind

1 cinnamon stick

1 tablespoon orange-flavoured
   liqueur

½ cup (75g) self-raising flour

2 tablespoons full-cream
   milk powder

1 tablespoon cocoa powder

125g (4 ounces) cream cheese,
   softened

24 chocolate-coated raisins

vegetable oil, for deep-frying

1 Stir the water, sugar, rind and cinnamon in medium saucepan over heat, without boiling, until sugar dissolves. Bring to the boil; boil, uncovered, without stirring, 5 minutes. Remove syrup from heat; stir in liqueur. Cool.

2 Sift flour, milk powder and cocoa into medium bowl; add cheese, mix to a soft dough with hand. Turn onto floured surface; knead 10 minutes. Roll one heaped teaspoon of dough around each chocolate raisin.

3 Heat oil in deep pan or wok; deep-fry balls, in batches, about 2 minutes or until browned. Drain on absorbent paper. Place gulab jaman in syrup; stand 1 hour before serving.

serves 8

chocolate gulab jaman with orange cinnamon syrup

2 eggs
2 egg yolks
⅓ cup (75g) caster
   (superfine) sugar
85g (3 ounces) dark eating
   (semi-sweet) chocolate, melted
1 cup (250ml) milk
1 cup (250ml) pouring cream
1 cup (120g) ground almonds
¼ cup (35g) plain
   (all-purpose) flour
1 tablespoon cocoa powder
425g (13½ ounces) canned
   seeded black cherries,
   drained
85g (3 ounces) dark eating
   (semi-sweet) chocolate,
   grated coarsely

1 Preheat oven to 180°C/350°F. Grease 23cm (9¼-inch) square slab cake pan.
2 Beat eggs, egg yolks and sugar in medium bowl with electric mixer until combined; beat in cooled, melted chocolate. Slowly beat in milk and cream. Stir in ground almonds, then sifted flour and cocoa.
3 Pour mixture into pan; sprinkle with cherries and grated chocolate.
4 Bake slice about 25 minutes. Stand slice 15 minutes; turn, top-side up, onto wire rack. Serve warm as a slice, or as a dessert with ice-cream or cream, if you like.

makes 20

black forest slice

white chocolate and passionfruit mousse eggs

We used six 6-hole (1-tablespoon/20ml) easter egg moulds for this recipe. Or, make eggs in six batches. You will need about 3 passionfruit for this recipe.

300g (9½ ounces) white chocolate Melts, melted
100g (3 ounces) white eating chocolate, chopped coarsely
20g (¾ ounce) unsalted butter
¼ cup (60ml) passionfruit pulp
1 egg, separated
⅔ cup (160ml) thickened (heavy) cream, whipped

1 Using small artist's brush, paint melted chocolate over inside of moulds (see page 232). Leave to set at room temperature. Gently remove eggs from moulds.
2 Meanwhile, stir chopped chocolate, butter and pulp in medium heatproof bowl over medium saucepan of simmering water until smooth. Stir in egg yolk. Cool.
3 Beat egg white in small bowl with electric mixer until soft peaks form. Fold egg white and cream into chocolate mixture, in two batches.
4 Divide mousse among eggs. Refrigerate 3 hours or overnight.
5 Serve drizzled with extra passionfruit pulp, if you like.

makes 36

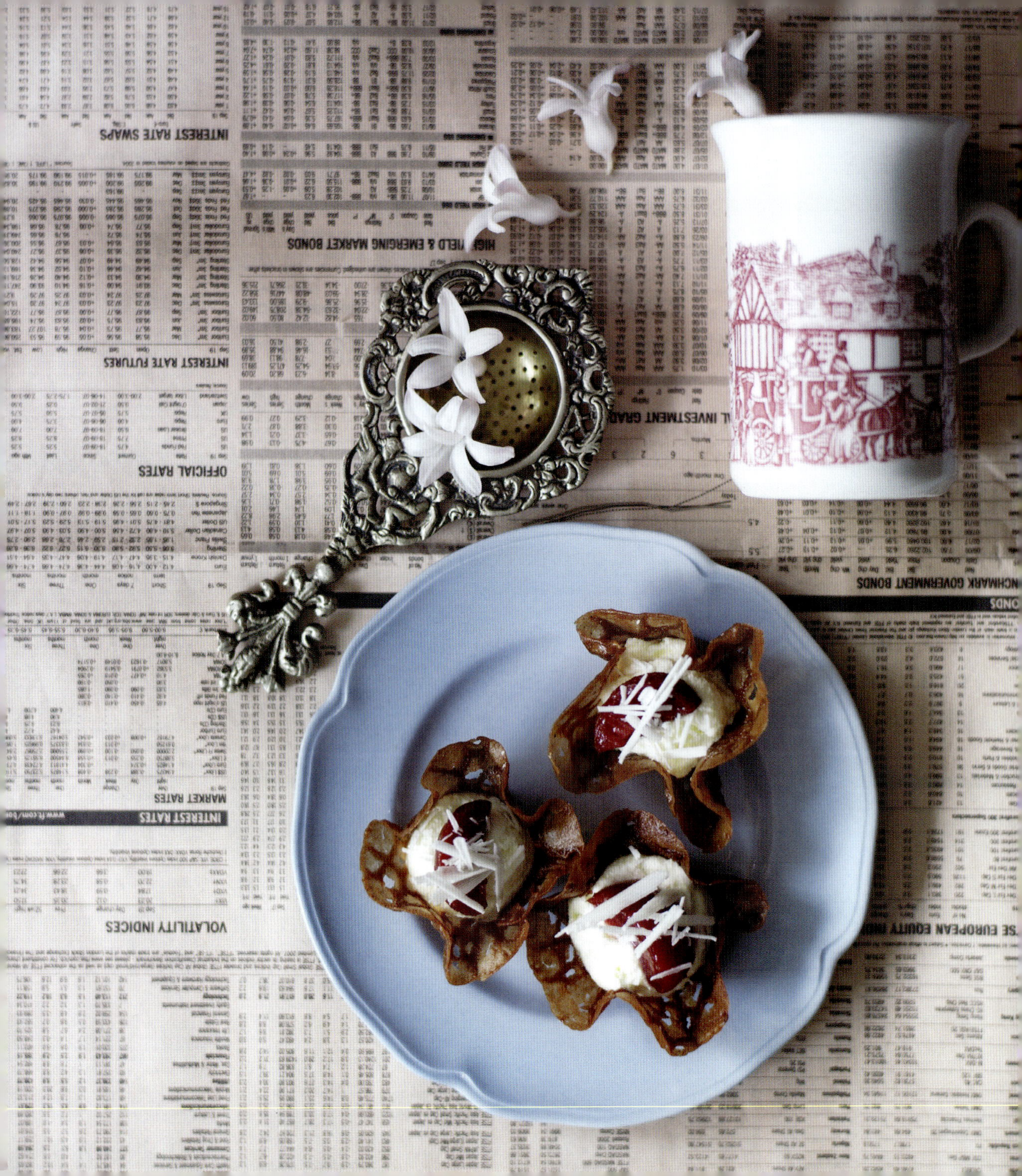

chocolate plum brandy baskets

50g (1½ ounces) white
chocolate Melts, melted
60g (2 ounces) butter
⅓ cup (75g) firmly packed
light brown sugar
2 tablespoons golden syrup
⅓ cup (50g) plain
(all-purpose) flour
1 teaspoon cocoa powder
1 teaspoon ground ginger
5 drained whole canned plums
(175g), seeded, quartered
white chocolate cream
½ cup (125ml) pouring cream
180g (5½ ounces) white eating
chocolate, chopped coarsely

1 Use white chocolate Melts to make curls (see page 230).
2 Make white chocolate cream.
3 Preheat oven to 180°C/350°F. Grease two oven trays; line with baking paper.
4 Stir butter, sugar and syrup in small saucepan over low heat until smooth. Remove from heat; stir in sifted flour, cocoa and ginger.
5 Drop rounded teaspoons of mixture about 5cm (2 inches) apart onto trays. (Until you master the handling and baking time of the snaps, bake only two at a time.) Bake about 7 minutes or until brandy snaps bubble; cool on tray 30 seconds.

6 Using metal spatula, quickly lift brandy snap from tray; shape each brandy snap into a basket-shape around base of 3cm (1¼-inch) glass. Cool each brandy snap for about 1 minute (see page 241); remove, place on wire rack to cool. Repeat with remaining mixture.
7 Just before serving, fill baskets with white chocolate cream. Top with plum pieces and white chocolate curls.
white chocolate cream Stir cream and chocolate in small heatproof bowl over small saucepan of simmering water until smooth. Cool; refrigerate 30 minutes or until spreadable. Beat chocolate mixture in small bowl with electric mixer until firm peaks form.

makes 18

chocolate fondants

These are the perfect do-ahead desserts; they can be frozen, ready-to-bake, weeks ahead. Make sure you're organised so the fondants are served and eaten while their centre is wonderfully soft and gooey.

200g (6½ ounces) dark eating (semi-sweet) chocolate, chopped coarsely
100g (3 ounces) unsalted butter, chopped coarsely
1 tablespoon cocoa powder
1 tablespoon self-raising flour
⅓ cup (75g) caster (superfine) sugar
3 eggs

1 Grease 6-hole (½-cup/125ml) friand pan evenly with a little melted butter.
2 Stir chocolate and butter in small heatproof bowl over small saucepan of simmering water until smooth.
3 Sift cocoa, flour and sugar into medium bowl; whisk in eggs and chocolate mixture.
4 Divide mixture among pan holes; cover pan with foil, freeze 3 hours or overnight.
5 Preheat oven to 220°C/425°F.
6 Bake frozen fondants 7 minutes; turn pan, bake further 7 minutes. Stand fondants 2 minutes; loosen edges with knife, gently ease out of pan. Serve immediately with cream or ice-cream, if you like.

makes 6

Rose, violet, nasturtium and pansy petals are all edible and make beautiful additions to recipes.

⅓ cup (75g) caster
   (superfine) sugar
¼ cup (42g) gelatine
3 cups (750ml) rosé wine
2 tablespoons pouring cream
100g (3 ounces) white eating
   chocolate, chopped coarsely
36 rose petals

rosé wine jellies

1 Sprinkle sugar and gelatine over 1 cup (250ml) of the wine in large heatproof jug; stand jug in medium saucepan of simmering water. Stir until gelatine dissolves.
2 Stir remaining wine into gelatine mixture. Pour mixture into two 18-hole (1-tablespoon/20ml) flexible jelly moulds. Refrigerate 3 hours or until firm.
3 Stir cream and chocolate in small heatproof bowl over small saucepan of simmering water until smooth. Refrigerate about 30 minutes, stirring occasionally, until spreadable.
4 Half-fill shallow baking dish with boiling water; stand jelly moulds in dish about 2 seconds or until jelly begins to come away from side of moulds. Carefully unmould jellies onto tray. Pipe or spoon chocolate mixture onto jellies; top with rose petals.

makes 36

100g (3 ounces) unsalted
  butter, softened
½ cup (80g) icing
  (confectioners') sugar
½ cup (140g) crunchy
  peanut butter
twelve 5cm x 9cm (2-inch x
  3¾-inch) ice-cream wafers
60g (2 ounces) dark eating
  (semi-sweet) chocolate,
  melted

peanut praline
⅓ cup (45g) roasted
  unsalted peanuts
½ cup (110g) caster
  (superfine) sugar
¼ cup (60ml) water

choc nut cream bites with peanut praline

1 Make peanut praline.
2 Beat butter and sifted icing sugar in small bowl with electric mixer until light and fluffy; beat in peanut butter.
3 Spread half the peanut butter mixture over four wafers. Top each with another wafer; spread remaining peanut butter mixture over the top of each sandwich. Top with remaining wafers to make four triple-decker wafer sandwiches. Refrigerate 1 hour.
4 Using serrated knife, cut wafer sandwiches crossways into four. Dip tops of sandwiches into chocolate; sprinkle with praline. Refrigerate until set.

peanut praline Place nuts on baking-paper-lined oven tray. Stir sugar and the water in small saucepan over heat, without boiling, until sugar dissolves. Bring to the boil; boil, uncovered, without stirring, until golden brown. Pour mixture over nuts; leave to set at room temperature. Break praline into small pieces.

makes 16

frozen chocolate tiramisu bars

½ cup (125ml) coffee-flavoured
  liqueur
2 large chocolate muffins
  (230g), crumbled
2 cups (500ml) coffee ice-cream,
  softened
180g (5½ ounces) dark eating
  (semi-sweet) chocolate,
  melted
2 tablespoons cocoa powder

1 Line 6-hole (⅔ cup/160ml) loaf pan with foil, extending foil 5cm (2 inches) over sides.
2 Sprinkle liqueur over muffins in medium bowl; stir in ice-cream.
3 Divide ice-cream mixture among pan holes, cover with foil; freeze about 3 hours or until firm.
4 Remove ice-cream bars from pan; remove foil, place bars on tray. Freeze ice-cream bars until required.
5 Trace 12cm x 15cm (4¾-inch x 6-inch) rectangle on piece of paper. Cover paper with plastic wrap. Spread one-sixth of the chocolate onto plastic wrap into rectangle shape. Remove one ice-cream bar from the freezer; stand in centre of chocolate rectangle. Pull plastic wrap up to encase bottom and sides of ice-cream bar (see page 231); return to tray, freeze 1 minute or until chocolate sets. Gently peel away plastic wrap (see page 231); return ice-cream bar to tray, freeze. Repeat with remaining chocolate and ice-cream bars.
6 Dust tiramisu bars with sifted cocoa; serve with a shot of hot coffee, if you like.

tip If chocolate starts to thicken between wrapping ice-cream bars, re-melt.

makes 6

white chocolate, rhubarb and ginger trifles

You will need about four large stems of rhubarb for this recipe.

2 cups (220g) coarsely chopped rhubarb
2 tablespoons caster (superfine) sugar
1 teaspoon finely grated orange rind
1 tablespoon orange juice
1 tablespoon finely chopped glacé ginger
12 gingernut biscuits (125g), chopped coarsely
1 cup (250ml) orange juice, extra
1 medium orange (240g), segmented (see page 242)
white chocolate cream
½ cup (125ml) pouring cream
180g (5½ ounces) white eating chocolate, chopped coarsely

1 Make white chocolate cream.
2 Combine rhubarb, sugar, rind and juice in small saucepan; bring to the boil. Reduce heat; simmer, uncovered, stirring occasionally, about 5 minutes or until rhubarb softens. Cool; stir in ginger.
3 Divide rhubarb mixture among six ⅔ cup (160ml) glasses; top with combined biscuits and extra juice, then white chocolate cream and orange segments.
white chocolate cream Stir cream and chocolate in small heatproof bowl over small saucepan of simmering water until smooth. Refrigerate about 30 minutes or until spreadable. Beat chocolate mixture with electric mixer until firm peaks form.

serves 6

iced coconut slice

You can use a 300ml carton of cream in this recipe.

4 egg yolks
2 tablespoons caster (superfine) sugar
100g (3 ounces) white eating chocolate, melted
⅓ cup (80ml) coconut-flavoured liqueur
2 egg whites
1¼ cups (310ml) pouring cream, whipped
1 small pineapple (900g), peeled, cored, chopped finely
½ cup finely shredded fresh mint
½ cup (125ml) pineapple juice

1 Line 14cm x 21cm (5½-inch x 8½-inch) loaf pan with strips of foil, extending foil 10cm (4 inches) over sides of pan.
2 Beat egg yolks and sugar in small bowl with electric mixer until thick and creamy; transfer mixture to large bowl. Stir in chocolate and liqueur.
3 Beat egg whites in small bowl with electric mixer until soft peaks form. Fold egg whites and cream into chocolate mixture, in two batches.
4 Pour mixture into pan; cover with foil, freeze overnight until firm.
5 Combine remaining ingredients in small bowl.
6 Serve pieces of slice topped with pineapple mixture.

serves 10

2 small apples (260g), peeled
4 sheets shortcrust pastry
⅓ cup (110g) chocolate
   hazelnut spread
1 egg white
1 tablespoon white sugar

1 Preheat oven to 200°C/400°F. Grease two oven trays; line with baking paper.
2 Cut each apple into eight wedges; remove cores.
3 Cut 16 x 10cm (4-inch) rounds from pastry sheets. Drop rounded teaspoons of spread into centre of each round; top each with an apple wedge. Brush edges with a little egg white; fold rounds in half to enclose filling, pinch edges to seal. Place on trays.
4 Brush turnovers with remaining egg white; sprinkle with sugar. Bake about 20 minutes. Transfer to wire rack to cool.

makes 16

choc-nut apple turnovers

2 medium pears (460g), peeled,
  cored, chopped finely
25g (¾ ounce) dark eating
  (semi-sweet) chocolate,
  chopped coarsely

mocha crumble

1 teaspoon instant coffee
  granules
½ teaspoon hot water
¼ cup (35g) plain
  (all-purpose) flour
1 tablespoon self-raising flour
2 tablespoons raw sugar
35g (1 ounce) unsalted butter,
  chopped
2 teaspoons cocoa powder

1 Make mocha crumble.
2 Preheat oven to 200°C/400°F.
Grease six ⅓ cup (80ml)
ovenproof dishes; place on
oven tray.
3 Divide pear and chocolate
among dishes; coarsely grate
crumble over pear mixture.
4 Bake about 20 minutes. Stand
5 minutes before serving with
cream or ice-cream, if you like.
mocha crumble Dissolve coffee
in the water in processor. Add
remaining ingredients; process
until combined. Wrap in plastic
wrap; freeze about 1 hour or
until firm.

serves 6

mocha pear crumble

chocolate pikelets with raspberry butter

1 cup (150g) self-raising flour
2 tablespoons cocoa powder
¼ cup (55g) caster
    (superfine) sugar
1 egg
1¼ cups (310ml) buttermilk
raspberry butter
1 cup (150g) frozen raspberries,
    thawed
150g (4½ ounces) unsalted
    butter, softened
⅔ cup (110g) icing
    (confectioners') sugar

1 Make raspberry butter.
2 Sift flour, cocoa and sugar into small bowl; whisk in egg and buttermilk.
3 Heat greased large heavy-based frying pan; drop tablespoons of batter into pan. Cook pikelets until bubbles appear on surface; turn pikelets with metal spatula to brown the other side.
4 Serve pikelets warm with raspberry butter and fresh raspberries, if you like.
raspberry butter Push raspberries through fine sieve into small bowl; discard seeds. Beat butter and sifted icing sugar in small bowl with electric mixer until light and fluffy. Beat in raspberry puree.

serves 6

chocomarmalaska

4 large chocolate muffins (460g)
⅓ cup (115g) orange marmalade
1 cup (250ml) chocolate ice-cream
3 egg whites
¾ cup (165g) firmly packed
   light brown sugar
1 teaspoon finely grated
   orange rind

1 Cut tops off muffins; discard. Hollow out muffin centres, leaving a 1cm (½-inch) border.
2 Drop level tablespoons of marmalade into each muffin. Top with ice-cream. Stand muffins on oven tray, freeze about 1 hour or until firm.
3 Preheat oven to 240°C/475°F.
4 Just before serving, beat egg whites in small bowl with electric mixer until soft peaks form; gradually add sugar, beating until dissolved between additions. Beat in rind.
5 Spread meringue over muffins. Bake about 2 minutes or until browned lightly. Serve immediately.

serves 4

chocolate pistachio tart

You could use a 22cm (8¾-inch) round loose-based fluted flan tin for this recipe.

½ cup (70g) roasted unsalted pistachios
100g (3 ounces) unsalted butter, softened
½ cup (110g) caster (superfine) sugar
2 eggs
⅔ cup (100g) self-raising flour
⅓ cup (35g) cocoa powder
½ cup (160g) raspberry jam (conserve)
12 roasted unsalted pistachios, extra
40g (1½ ounces) dark chocolate Melts, melted
pastry
1¼ cups (185g) plain (all-purpose) flour
½ cup (80g) icing (confectioners') sugar
125g (4 ounces) cold unsalted butter, chopped coarsely
2 tablespoons iced water, approximately

1 Make pastry.
2 Grease 12.5cm x 35cm (5-inch x 14-inch) loose-based fluted flan tin. Reserve one-quarter of the dough for decoration. Roll remaining dough between sheets of baking paper until large enough to line tin. Ease dough into tin; press into base and sides. Trim edges; prick base all over with fork. Refrigerate 30 minutes.
3 Roll out reserved dough on floured surface, cut out 12 x 2cm (¾-inch) rounds from reserved dough; place on baking-paper-lined tray. Refrigerate 30 minutes.
4 Preheat oven to 200°C/400°F.
5 Blend or process nuts finely.
6 Beat butter and sugar in small bowl with electric mixer until light and fluffy. Beat in eggs, one at a time. Transfer mixture to medium bowl; stir in sifted flour and cocoa, and nuts. Spread jam over base of pastry case; top with pistachio filling. Top filling with pastry rounds. Bake 15 minutes.

7 Reduce oven to 180°C/350°F; bake further 25 minutes. Cool.
8 Dip extra nuts in chocolate; place on pastry rounds. Cool before slicing.
pastry Process sifted flour and sugar with butter until crumbly. Add enough of the water until ingredients just come together when processed. Knead dough on floured surface until smooth. Cover; refrigerate 30 minutes.

serves 16

rum and raisin chocolate mousse eggs

We used six 6-hole (1-tablespoon/ 20ml) easter egg moulds for this recipe. Or, make eggs in six batches.

300g (9½ ounces) dark
  chocolate Melts, melted
1 cup (160g) coarsely chopped
  raisins
⅓ cup (80ml) dark rum
100g (3 ounces) milk eating
  chocolate, chopped coarsely
20g (¾ ounce) unsalted butter
1 egg, separated
⅔ cup (160ml) thickened (heavy)
  cream, whipped

1 Using small artist's brush, paint dark chocolate over inside of moulds (see page 232). Leave to set at room temperature. Gently remove eggs from mould.
2 Combine raisins and half the rum in small bowl.
3 Stir milk chocolate, butter and remaining rum in medium heatproof bowl over medium saucepan of simmering water until smooth. Stir in egg yolk; cool.
4 Beat egg white in small bowl with electric mixer until soft peaks form. Fold egg white and cream into chocolate mixture, in two batches.
5 Divide raisin mixture among chocolate eggs; top with mousse. Refrigerate 3 hours or overnight.
6 Serve with dark chocolate curls (see page 230), if you like.

makes 36

opera gateau

4 eggs
1¼ cups (150g) ground almonds
1 cup (160g) icing
(confectioners') sugar
⅓ cup (50g) plain
(all-purpose) flour
25g (¾ ounce) unsalted
butter, melted
4 egg whites
1 tablespoon caster
(superfine) sugar

coffee butter cream
¼ cup (60ml) milk
¼ cup (55g) light brown sugar
2 teaspoons instant
coffee granules
1 egg yolk
125g (4 ounces) unsalted
butter, softened

coffee syrup
⅓ cup (80ml) boiling water
2 tablespoons caster
(superfine) sugar
1 tablespoon instant
coffee granules

ganache
160g (5 ounces) dark eating
(semi-sweet) chocolate,
chopped coarsely
⅓ cup (80ml) pouring cream

glaze
50g (1½ ounces) unsalted butter
75g (2½ ounces) dark eating
(semi-sweet) chocolate

1 Preheat oven to 220°C/425°F. Grease two 25cm x 30cm (10-inch x 12-inch) swiss roll pans; line bases with baking paper, extending paper 5cm (2 inches) over long sides.
2 Beat eggs, ground almonds and sifted icing sugar in small bowl with electric mixer until creamy; beat in flour. Transfer mixture to large bowl; stir in butter.
3 Beat egg whites in small bowl with electric mixer until soft peaks form; add caster sugar, beating until sugar dissolves. Fold into almond mixture, in two batches.
4 Divide mixture between pans. Bake about 7 minutes. Cool.
5 Make coffee butter cream, coffee syrup and ganache.
6 Cut each cake into a 20cm x 25cm (8-inch x 10-inch) rectangle and a 10cm x 25cm (4-inch x 10-inch) rectangle (see page 242).
7 Place one of the large cake rectangles on baking-paper-lined tray; brush with half the coffee syrup. Spread cake with half the butter cream; refrigerate 10 minutes. Top butter cream with the two small cake rectangles, side-by-side. Brush with the remaining coffee syrup; spread with ganache. Top with remaining

cake; refrigerate 10 minutes. Spread top of cake with remaining butter cream; refrigerate 3 hours (see page 242).
8 Meanwhile, make glaze.
9 Working quickly, spread glaze evenly over cake. Refrigerate 30 minutes or until glaze has set.
coffee butter cream Stir milk, sugar and coffee in small saucepan, over low heat, until sugar dissolves. Whisk egg yolk in small bowl; gradually whisk in hot milk mixture. Return custard to pan; stir over heat, without boiling, about 5 minutes or until thickened slightly. Cool. Beat butter in small bowl with electric mixer until light and fluffy; beat in custard.
coffee syrup Stir ingredients in small bowl.
ganache Stir ingredients in small heatproof bowl over small saucepan of simmering water until smooth. Refrigerate until spreadable.
glaze Stir ingredients in small heatproof bowl over small saucepan of simmering water until smooth. Use while warm.

serves 24

250g (8 ounces) dark eating (semi-sweet) chocolate, melted

1¼ cups (135g) coarsely chopped roasted walnuts

150g (4½ ounces) dark eating (semi-sweet) chocolate, chopped coarsely

¾ cup (165g) firmly packed light brown sugar

3 eggs

1 Grease 19cm x 29cm (7¾-inch x 11¾-inch) slice pan; line base and sides with foil, extending foil 5cm (2 inches) over long sides.
2 Spread melted chocolate over base of pan; refrigerate until set.
3 Preheat oven to 180°C/350°F.
4 Process nuts, chopped chocolate, sugar and eggs until combined. Pour nut mixture over chocolate base. Bake about 20 minutes. Cool.
5 Remove from pan; carefully remove foil. Cut into squares.

makes 24

decadent double-choc slice

white chocolate lamingtons

6 eggs
⅔ cup (150g) caster
   (superfine) sugar
80g (2½ ounces) white eating
   chocolate, chopped finely
½ cup (75g) plain
   (all-purpose) flour
⅓ cup (50g) self-raising flour
⅓ cup (50g) cornflour
   (cornstarch)
4 cups (640g) icing
   (confectioners') sugar
¾ cup (180ml) milk
2 cups (150g) shredded coconut
100g (3 ounces) white eating
   chocolate, grated finely

1 Preheat oven to 180°C/350°F. Grease 23cm (9¼-inch) square slab cake pan; line base and sides with baking paper, extending paper 5cm (2 inches) over sides.
2 Beat eggs in medium bowl with electric mixer about 10 minutes or until thick and creamy; gradually beat in caster sugar, dissolving between each addition. Fold in chopped chocolate and triple-sifted flours.
3 Spread mixture into pan; bake about 35 minutes. Turn cake immediately onto baking-paper-lined wire rack to cool; refrigerate while preparing the icing.

4 Sift icing sugar into medium heatproof bowl; stir in milk. Place bowl over medium saucepan of simmering water, stir until icing is of a coating consistency.
5 Cut cold cake into 25 squares.
6 Dip each square of cake into icing, drain off excess. Toss squares in combined coconut and grated chocolate. Place lamingtons on wire rack to set.

makes 25

mini choc-chip banana loaves

1 cup (460g) mashed
  overripe banana
¾ cup (165g) firmly packed
  light brown sugar
2 eggs
60g (2 ounces) butter, melted
¼ cup (60ml) buttermilk
⅔ cup (100g) self-raising flour
⅔ cup (100g) wholemeal
  self-raising flour
½ cup (95g) milk Choc Bits

1 Preheat oven to 180°C/350°F.
Grease 8-hole (¾ cup/180ml)
mini loaf pan; line base and two
short sides with baking paper.
2 Combine banana and sugar
in large bowl; stir in eggs,
butter and buttermilk, then
sifted flours and Choc Bits.
3 Divide mixture among pan
holes; bake about 20 minutes.
Stand loaves 5 minutes; turn,
top-side up, onto wire rack to
cool. Serve warm with butter,
if you like.

makes 8

toffee chocolate spoons

1 cup (220g) caster
   (superfine) sugar
½ cup (125ml) water
100g (3 ounces) milk eating
   chocolate, melted

1 Line two oven trays with baking paper.
2 Combine sugar and the water in small saucepan; stir over heat, without boiling, until sugar dissolves. Bring to the boil. Reduce heat; simmer, uncovered, without stirring, until toffee is golden brown. Remove from heat; stand 2 minutes.
3 Spoon toffee onto trays into 10 x 14cm (5½-inch) spoon shapes; allow to set at room temperature.
4 Dip toffee spoons into chocolate; return to trays. Set at room temperature.
5 Use spoons to stir through mugs of hot milk to make hot chocolate, if you like.

makes 10

black forest chocolate boxes

2 tablespoons cocoa powder
2 tablespoons water
70g (2½ ounces) dark eating
  (semi-sweet) chocolate,
  melted
70g (2½ ounces) butter, melted
⅔ cup (150g) firmly packed
  light brown sugar
½ cup (60g) ground almonds
2 eggs, separated
200g (6½ ounces) dark eating
  (semi-sweet) chocolate,
  melted, extra
425g (13½ ounces) canned
  seeded black cherries
1 teaspoon cornflour
  (cornstarch)
1 tablespoon kirsch
⅓ cup (110g) cherry jam
  (conserve), warmed, sieved
kirsch cream
250g (8 ounces) mascarpone
  cheese
2 tablespoons icing
  (confectioners') sugar
1 tablespoon kirsch

1 Preheat oven to 160°C/325°F.
Grease deep 23cm (9¼-inch)
square cake pan; line with
baking paper, extending paper
5cm (2 inches) over sides.
2 Blend sifted cocoa with the
water in large bowl until smooth.
Stir in chocolate, butter, sugar,
ground almonds and egg yolks.
3 Beat egg whites in small bowl
with electric mixer until soft peaks
form; fold into chocolate mixture.
4 Pour mixture into pan; bake
about 40 minutes. Stand cake
10 minutes; turn, top-side up,
onto wire rack to cool.
5 Trim cake to 20cm (8-inch)
square. Cover; freeze cake
30 minutes or until firm. Cut cake
into 16 x 5cm (2-inch) squares.
6 Line a flat tray with baking
paper. Spread extra chocolate
into 32cm (12¾-inch) square;
set at room temperature. Cut
chocolate to 30cm (12-inch)
square; cut square into 36 x 5cm
(2-inch) squares, then cut each
square in half to give 72 rectangles.
Refrigerate 10 minutes.

7 Drain cherries; reserve syrup.
Blend cornflour with 1 tablespoon
of the syrup in small saucepan.
Stir in remaining syrup and
liqueur; cook, stirring, until
mixture boils and thickens.
Reduce heat; simmer cherry
glaze, stirring, 1 minute. Cool.
8 Make kirsch cream.
9 Brush edges of cake squares
with jam; press chocolate
rectangles onto sides of cakes
(see page 231). (You will have
leftover chocolate rectangles.)
Spoon kirsch cream into centre
of cakes; top with cherries and
cherry glaze.
kirsch cream Combine
ingredients in small bowl.

makes 16

90g (3 ounces) white eating
  chocolate, chopped coarsely
90g (3 ounces) unsalted butter,
  chopped coarsely
½ cup (110g) firmly packed
  light brown sugar
2 tablespoons golden syrup
½ cup (125ml) milk
¾ cup (110g) plain
  (all-purpose) flour
¼ cup (35g) self-raising flour
1 egg
2 tablespoons milk Choc Bits
1 tablespoon icing
  (confectioners') sugar

1 Preheat oven to 160°C/325°F. Grease 9-hole (½ cup/125ml) friand pan; line bases with baking paper.
2 Stir chocolate, butter, brown sugar, syrup and milk in medium saucepan, over low heat, until smooth. Cool 15 minutes.
3 Whisk in sifted flours and egg. Stir in Choc Bits. Divide mixture among pan holes.
4 Bake cakes about 25 minutes. Stand cakes 5 minutes; turn, top-side up, onto wire rack to cool. Serve dusted with sifted icing sugar.

makes 9

caramel choc-chip mud cakes

180g (5½ ounces) white eating
   chocolate, melted
1¼ cups (95g) shredded
   coconut
silver cachous (dragees)

1 Line two trays with baking paper.
2 Combine chocolate and coconut in medium bowl. Drop heaped tablespoons of mixture onto trays; shape mixture into wreaths using the end of a wooden spoon to make holes in the centre of each wreath.
3 Decorate wreaths with cachous. Refrigerate until set. Tie with ribbon, if you like.

makes 8

coconut christmas wreaths

white chocolate and raspberry mille-feuilles

1 sheet puff pastry
50g (1½ ounces) white eating
  chocolate, melted
1 tablespoon raspberry jam
  (conserve)
½ cup (125ml) thickened
  (heavy) cream
50g (1½ ounces) white eating
  chocolate, grated finely
60g (2 ounces) fresh raspberries
30g (1 ounce) white eating
  chocolate, chopped coarsely
1 tablespoon thickened
  (heavy) cream, extra
1 tablespoon icing
  (confectioners') sugar

1 Preheat oven to 240°C/475°F. Grease oven tray.
2 Place pastry sheet on tray; place a second oven tray on top. Bake about 15 minutes or until pastry is browned and crisp. Cool 2 minutes.
3 Spread pastry sheet with melted chocolate, then jam. Cut into 18 rectangles.
4 Beat cream in small bowl with electric mixer until firm peaks form; fold in grated chocolate.
5 Spread cream mixture over jam; sandwich pastry rectangles with raspberries.
6 Stir chopped chocolate and extra cream in small heatproof bowl over small saucepan of simmering water until smooth.
7 Drizzle mille-feuilles with chocolate mixture; dust with sifted icing sugar.

makes 9

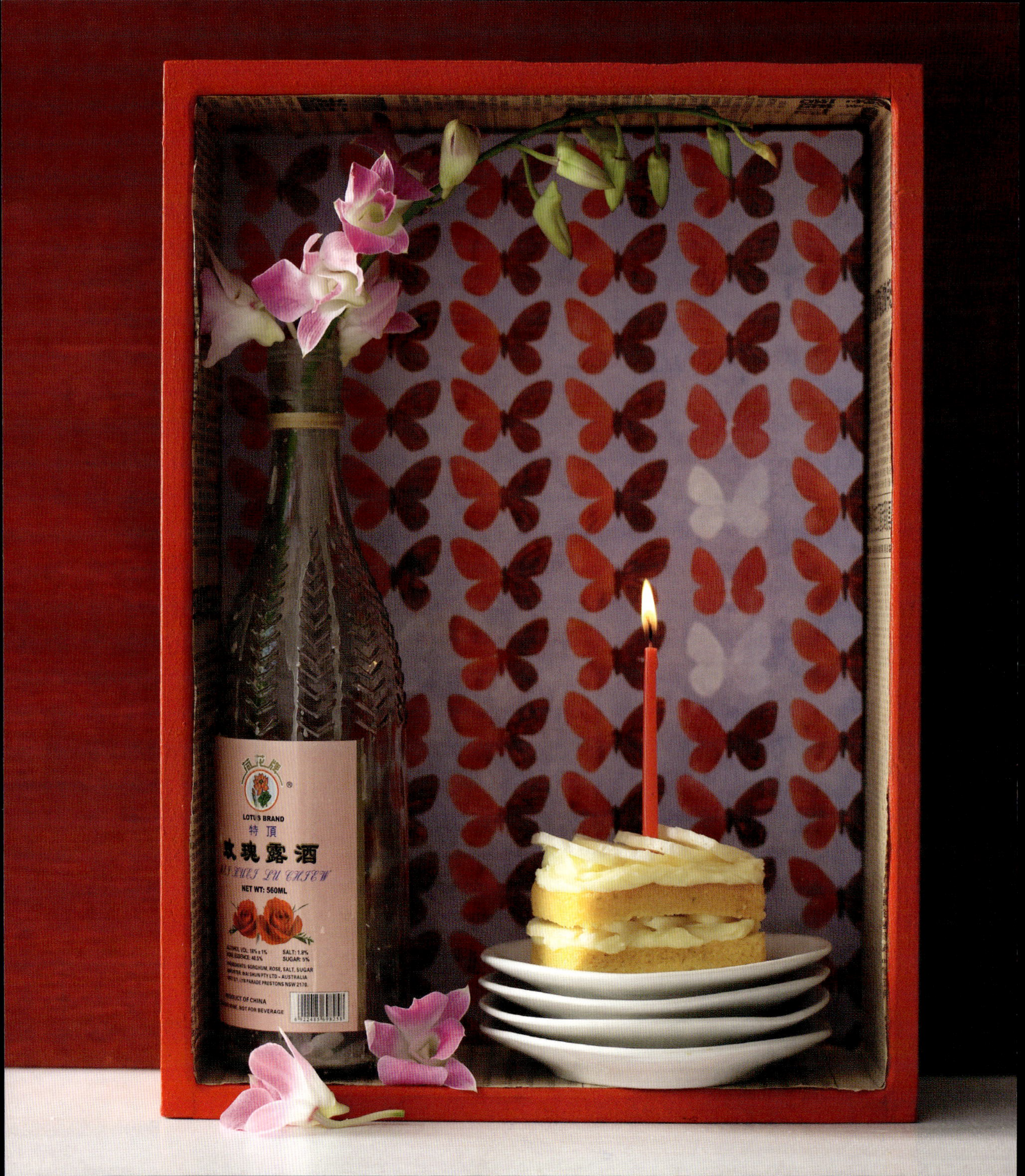
LOTUS BRAND
特頂
玫瑰露酒
NET WT: 560ML
SALT: 1.8%
SUGAR: 5%

lime and pineapple loaves

100g (3 ounces) unsalted
  butter, softened
1 tablespoon finely grated
  lime rind
½ cup (110g) caster
  (superfine) sugar
2 eggs
¾ cup (110g) self-raising flour
2 tablespoons milk
½ small pineapple (450g), peeled,
  cored, sliced thinly
lime ganache
180g (5½ ounces) white eating
  chocolate, chopped coarsely
2 tablespoons lime juice
¼ cup (60ml) pouring cream

1 Preheat oven to 150°C/300°F.
Grease 8-hole (¾ cup/180ml)
mini loaf pan; line bases with
baking paper.
2 Beat butter, rind, sugar, eggs,
flour and milk in medium bowl
with electric mixer, on low speed,
until combined. Increase speed
to medium; beat about 3 minutes
or until mixture is light and fluffy.
Divide mixture among pan holes;
cover pan loosely with foil. Bake
about 25 minutes. Stand cakes
5 minutes; turn, top-side up,
onto wire rack to cool.
3 Meanwhile, make lime ganache.
4 Split loaves in half. Sandwich
loaves with half of the ganache
and half of the pineapple. Top
loaves with remaining ganache
and pineapple.

lime ganache Stir chocolate, juice
and cream in small heatproof bowl
over small saucepan of simmering
water until smooth. Refrigerate
until spreadable.

makes 8

white choc-chip orange and cranberry mini muffins

2 cups (300g) self-raising flour
½ cup (110g) caster
   (superfine) sugar
¾ cup (135g) white Choc Bits
½ cup (65g) dried cranberries
60g (2 ounces) butter, melted
¾ cup (180ml) milk
1 egg
2 teaspoons finely grated
   orange rind
¼ cup (60ml) orange juice
cranberry icing
1½ cups (240g) icing
   (confectioners') sugar
½ teaspoon vegetable oil
2 tablespoons cranberry juice,
   approximately

1 Preheat oven to 200°C/400°F. Line four 12-hole (1-tablespoon/20ml) mini muffin pans with paper cases.
2 Sift dry ingredients into medium bowl; stir in remaining ingredients.
3 Divide mixture among cases. Bake about 10 minutes. Stand muffins 2 minutes; turn, top-side up, onto wire rack to cool.
4 Meanwhile, make cranberry icing. Spread muffins with icing.
cranberry icing Sift icing sugar into small heatproof bowl. Stir in oil and enough juice to make a paste. Stir over small saucepan of simmering water until icing is spreadable.

makes 48

milk chocolate custard tarts

You can use a 300ml carton
of cream in this recipe.

⅓ cup (75g) caster
   (superfine) sugar
2 tablespoons cornflour
   (cornstarch)
1¼ cups (310ml) pouring cream
100g (3 ounces) milk eating
   chocolate, chopped coarsely
4 egg yolks
1 sheet butter puff pastry
1 tablespoon icing
   (confectioners') sugar

1 Preheat oven to 220°C/425°F.
Grease two 12-hole (1-tablespoon/
20ml) mini muffin pans.
2 Combine caster sugar and
cornflour in small saucepan;
stir in cream. Cook, stirring,
until mixture boils and thickens.
Reduce heat; simmer, stirring,
1 minute. Remove pan from
heat. Add chocolate and egg
yolks; stir until smooth.
3 Cut pastry sheet in half; stack
pastry halves on top of each
other. Roll pastry up tightly from
short side; cut into 24 x 5mm
(¼-inch) thick slices.
4 Roll slices between sheets of
baking paper into 8cm (3¼-inch)
rounds; press rounds into
pan holes.
5 Divide custard among pastry
cases. Bake about 10 minutes.
Stand tarts 5 minutes; serve
warm tarts dusted with sifted
icing sugar.

makes 24

mocha cream hearts

You can use a 300ml carton of cream in this recipe.

50g (1½ ounces) unsalted butter
½ cup (125ml) water
½ cup (75g) plain
   (all-purpose) flour
2 teaspoons cocoa powder
2 eggs
150g (4½ ounces) milk eating
   chocolate, melted
mocha cream
2 teaspoons instant
   coffee granules
1 teaspoon hot water
1¼ cups (310ml) thickened
   (heavy) cream
¼ cup (40g) icing
   (confectioners') sugar

1 Preheat oven to 200°C/400°F. Grease oven tray. Trace eight 7cm (3-inch) hearts onto a piece of baking paper to use as a guide; line tray with paper.
2 Combine butter and the water in medium saucepan; bring to the boil. Add sifted flour and cocoa; beat with wooden spoon over high heat until mixture comes away from base and side of pan to form a smooth ball. Transfer mixture to small bowl; beat in eggs, one at a time, with electric mixer until mixture becomes glossy.
3 Spoon mixture into piping bag fitted with a 5mm (¼-inch) plain tube. Pipe half of the mixture into eight hearts on tray, using paper as a guide. Pipe remaining mixture directly on top of previous hearts. (See page 233.)
4 Bake hearts 7 minutes.

5 Reduce oven to180°C/350°F; bake hearts about 10 minutes or until crisp. Remove from oven. Using serrated knife, split hearts in half, return to trays. Bake about 10 minutes or until dried out.
6 Meanwhile, make mocha cream.
7 Place half of the hearts, top-side up, on a wire rack over tray; spread with chocolate. Leave to set at room temperature. (See page 233.)
8 Fill remaining hearts with mocha cream; top with chocolate coated hearts (see page 233).
mocha cream Dissolve coffee in the water; cool. Beat cream, sifted icing sugar and coffee mixture in small bowl with electric mixer until firm peaks form.

makes 8

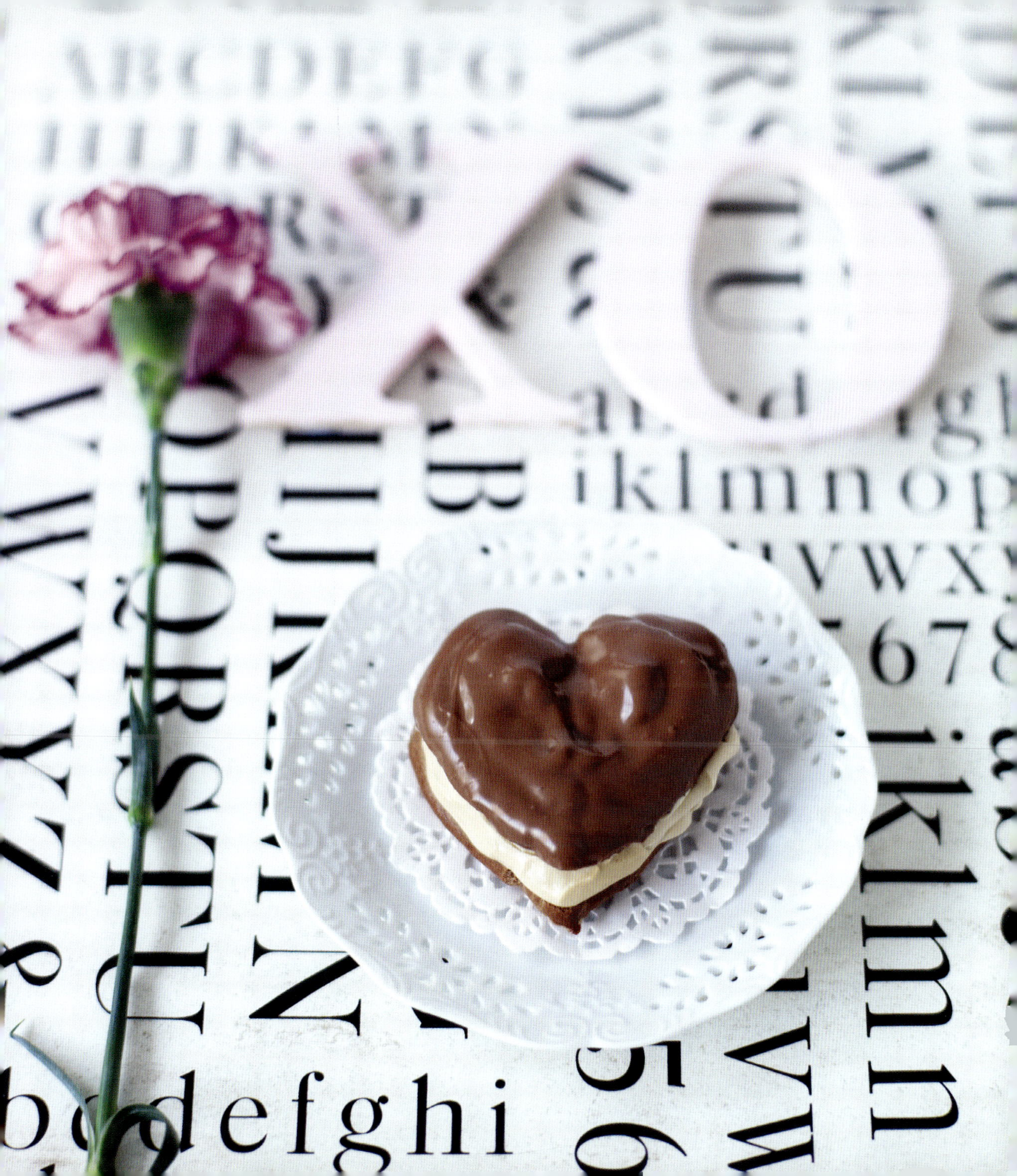
XO
iklmnop

1 tablespoon anise seeds
200g (6½ ounce) dark eating
   (semi-sweet) chocolate,
   melted
¾ cup (120g) finely chopped
   dried pears
½ cup (65g) finely chopped
   roasted macadamias

1 Dry-fry anise in small frying pan until fragrant; chop finely.
2 Warm a tray on stove top or in oven; cover with baking paper.
3 Combine anise with remaining ingredients in medium bowl.
4 Spread chocolate mixture onto tray as thinly as possible; refrigerate until set.
5 Break bark into rough pieces. Serve with coffee or ice-cream, if you like.

spicy fruit and nut bark

cinnamon prune swirls

1 seeded prune, chopped finely
1 tablespoon chocolate-
  flavoured liqueur
20 x 3cm (1¼-inch) milk
  chocolate pastilles
whipped cinnamon ganache
100g (3 ounces) milk eating
  chocolate, chopped coarsely
2 tablespoons pouring cream
¼ teaspoon ground cinnamon

1 Make whipped cinnamon ganache.
2 Meanwhile, combine prune and liqueur in small saucepan; stir over low heat until the liqueur has been absorbed. Cool.
3 Spoon ganache into piping bag fitted with small fluted tube. Pipe swirls of ganache onto pastilles; top with a piece of prune.

whipped cinnamon ganache
Stir chocolate, cream and cinnamon in small heatproof bowl over small saucepan of simmering water until smooth. Remove from heat; cool. Beat chocolate mixture in small bowl with electric mixer until spreadable.

makes 20

chocolate and raspberry tarts

125g (4 ounces) unsalted butter
½ cup (50g) cocoa powder
⅓ cup (110g) raspberry jam
(conserve)
⅔ cup (150g) caster
(superfine) sugar
2 eggs, beaten lightly
⅔ cup (100g) plain
(all-purpose) flour
pinch bicarbonate of
(baking) soda
125g (4 ounces) cream cheese,
softened
1 egg yolk
½ cup (75g) frozen raspberries

1 Preheat oven to 160°C/325°F. Grease six 10cm (4-inch) round, loose-based flan tins; place on oven tray.
2 Melt butter in medium saucepan. Add sifted cocoa; whisk over low heat until mixture boils. Remove from heat; whisk in jam and ½ cup of the sugar. Stir in eggs, then sifted flour and soda. Divide mixture among tins.
3 Beat cheese, remaining sugar and egg yolk in small bowl with electric mixer until smooth; stir in raspberries.
4 Drop spoonfuls of cheese mixture over chocolate mixture; pull a knife backwards and forwards several times for marbled effect. Bake about 30 minutes. Serve tarts warm or cold with whipped cream, if you like.

makes 6

milk chocolate praline eggs

We used Kinder Surprise chocolate eggs available in most supermarkets.

12 x 20g (¾-ounce) hollow chocolate eggs
200g (6½ ounces) milk eating chocolate, chopped coarsely
½ cup (125ml) pouring cream
praline
⅓ cup (45g) coarsely chopped roasted hazelnuts
⅓ cup (55g) coarsely chopped roasted almonds
½ cup (110g) caster (superfine) sugar
2 tablespoons water

1 Make praline.
2 Carefully cut tops from chocolate eggs; discard tops.
3 Stir chocolate and cream in small heatproof bowl over small saucepan of simmering water until smooth; cool. Stir praline into chocolate mixture. Refrigerate until spreadable.
4 Place chocolate eggs, cut-side up, in egg cups. Spoon chocolate praline mixture into eggs.
praline Place nuts on baking-paper-lined oven tray. Combine sugar and the water in small saucepan; stir over heat, without boiling, until sugar dissolves. Bring to the boil; boil, uncovered, until toffee is golden brown. Pour toffee over nuts; leave to set at room temperature. Break praline into pieces; process until chopped finely.

makes 12

⅓ cup (75g) caster
  (superfine) sugar
2 tablespoons water
⅔ cup (160ml) pouring cream
200g (6½ ounces) dark eating
  (semi-sweet) chocolate,
  chopped coarsely
1 teaspoon sea salt flakes
200g (6½ ounces) milk eating
  chocolate, melted

salted caramel truffles

1 Combine sugar and the water in small saucepan; stir over heat, without boiling, until sugar dissolves. Bring to the boil; boil, uncovered, without stirring, until golden brown. Add cream; stir over low heat until toffee pieces melt. Remove from heat; stir in dark chocolate and half of the salt until smooth. Refrigerate mixture overnight.
2 Working with a quarter of the chocolate mixture at a time (keep remainder refrigerated), roll rounded teaspoons of mixture into balls; place on foil-lined tray. Freeze until firm.
3 Working quickly, using two forks, dip truffles in milk chocolate (see page 232). Return truffles to tray; sprinkle with remaining salt. Refrigerate truffles until firm.

makes 25

2 eggs, separated
1 tablespoon caster
   (superfine) sugar
50g (1½ ounces) dark eating
   (semi-sweet) chocolate,
   melted
2 tablespoons mint-flavoured
   liqueur
⅔ cup (160ml) pouring cream
8 paddle-pop sticks

1 Beat egg yolks and sugar in small bowl with electric mixer until thick and creamy; beat in chocolate and liqueur. Transfer to medium bowl.
2 Beat cream in small bowl with electric mixer until soft peaks form; fold into chocolate mixture.
3 Beat egg whites in small bowl with electric mixer until soft peaks form; fold into chocolate mixture.
4 Pour mixture into eight ¼ cup (60ml) ice-block moulds; push paddle-pop sticks into centre of each mould. Press lids on firmly; freeze overnight.

makes 8

after dinner mint ices

dark chocolate pistachio brittle

2 cups (440g) caster (superfine) sugar
½ cup (125ml) water
1 cup (140g) roasted pistachios, chopped coarsely
200g (6½ ounces) dark eating (semi-sweet) chocolate, melted

1 Line oven tray with baking paper.
2 Combine sugar and the water in medium saucepan; stir over heat, without boiling, until sugar dissolves. Bring to the boil; boil, uncovered, without stirring, until golden brown. Allow bubbles to subside; add nuts. Pour mixture onto tray; leave to set at room temperature.
3 Spread chocolate over brittle; refrigerate about 10 minutes or until chocolate sets. Break brittle into pieces.

serves 15

chocolate, lemon and thyme truffles

250g (8 ounces) white eating
  chocolate, chopped coarsely
¼ cup (60ml) pouring cream
1 teaspoon finely grated
  lemon rind
1 tablespoon lemon juice
½ teaspoon finely chopped
  fresh thyme leaves
250g (8 ounces) white eating
  chocolate, melted
2 teaspoons finely grated
  lemon rind, extra

1 Stir chopped chocolate, cream, rind and juice in small heatproof bowl over small saucepan of simmering water until smooth. Remove from heat; stir in thyme. Refrigerate mixture overnight.
2 Working with a quarter of the chocolate mixture at a time (keep remainder refrigerated), roll rounded teaspoons of mixture into balls; place on foil-lined tray. Freeze until firm.
3 Working quickly, using two forks, dip truffles in melted chocolate (see page 232). Return truffles to tray; sprinkle with extra rind. Refrigerate truffles until firm.

makes 25

milk chocolate beetroot cake

3 small beetroot (300g), peeled
250g (8 ounces) butter, softened
1 cup (220g) caster
   (superfine) sugar
4 eggs
1 cup (150g) plain (all-purpose)
   flour
1 cup (150g) self-raising flour
¼ cup (25g) cocoa powder
100g (3 ounces) milk eating
   chocolate, chopped coarsely
fluffy chocolate ganache
200g (6½ ounces) dark eating
   (semi-sweet) chocolate,
   chopped coarsely
½ cup (125ml) pouring cream

1 Preheat oven to 180°C/350°F.
Grease 20cm x 30cm (8-inch x
12-inch) lamington pan; line with
baking paper, extending paper
5cm (2 inches) over long sides.
2 Grate beetroot coarsely.
3 Beat butter and sugar in small
bowl with electric mixer until light
and fluffy. Beat in eggs, one at a
time. Stir in sifted flours and cocoa,
then chocolate and beetroot.
4 Spread mixture into pan;
bake about 40 minutes. Stand
cake 5 minutes; turn, top-side
up, onto wire rack to cool.
5 Meanwhile, make fluffy
chocolate ganache.
6 Spread cake with ganache.
fluffy chocolate ganache Stir
ingredients in small heatproof
bowl over small saucepan of
simmering water until smooth;
cool. Refrigerate until spreadable.

serves 20

50g (1½ ounces) dark eating
(semi-sweet) chocolate,
chopped coarsely
2 tablespoons raspberry-
flavoured liqueur
1 medium pear (230g),
chopped finely
½ cup (125ml) vanilla ice-cream

1 Stir chocolate and liqueur in
small heatproof bowl over small
saucepan of simmering water
until smooth.
2 Divide half of the chocolate
mixture among six ⅓ cup (80ml)
glasses. Top with half of the
pear, half of the ice-cream and
remaining chocolate mixture.
Top with remaining ice-cream
and pear.

serves 6

chocolate and pear shots

praline rocky road ice-cream

2 cups (500ml) chocolate
  ice-cream, softened
½ cup (125g) coarsely chopped
  glacé peaches
¾ cup (90g) coarsely chopped
  roasted pecans
coconut praline
⅔ cup (150g) caster
  (superfine) sugar
2 tablespoons water
½ cup (40g) toasted shredded
  coconut

1 Combine ice-cream, peaches and nuts in large bowl. Freeze until almost firm.

2 Meanwhile, make coconut praline.

3 Stir praline through ice-cream mixture. Spread mixture into 15cm x 25cm (6-inch x 10-inch) loaf pan, cover with foil; freeze until firm.

4 Serve scoops of ice-cream sprinkled with dark chocolate curls (see page 230), if you like.

coconut praline Line oven tray with baking paper. Combine sugar and the water in medium saucepan; stir over heat, without boiling, until sugar dissolves. Bring to the boil; boil, uncovered, without stirring, until golden brown. Stir in coconut. Pour mixture onto tray; set at room temperature. Chop coarsely.

serves 4

crunchy bubble bars

4 cups (180g) coco pops
250g (8 ounces) dark eating
   (semi-sweet) chocolate,
   chopped coarsely
100g (3 ounces) butter,
   chopped coarsely
¼ cup (60ml) light corn syrup

1 Grease 20cm x 30cm (8-inch x
12-inch) lamington pan; line with
baking paper, extending paper
5cm (2 inches) over long sides.
2 Process half of the coco pops
until coarse.
3 Stir chocolate, butter and syrup
in large heatproof bowl over
large saucepan of simmering
water until smooth. Remove
from heat; stir in all coco pops.
4 Spread mixture into pan;
refrigerate until set. Cut into bars.

makes 40

raspberry rapture ice-cream cakes

2 cups (500ml) raspberry
  ice-cream, softened
180g (5½ ounces) white eating
  chocolate, melted
pink food colouring
450g (14½ ounces) madeira cake
¼ cup (80g) raspberry jam
  (conserve)

1 Grease 15cm x 25cm (6-inch x 10-inch) loaf pan; line with baking paper, extending paper 5cm (2 inches) over long sides.
2 Spread ice-cream into pan, cover with foil; freeze until firm.
3 Remove ice-cream from pan. Cut six 6.5cm (2¾-inch) hearts from ice-cream; place hearts on baking-paper-lined tray, cover with foil; freeze until firm.
4 Line another tray with baking paper. Tint melted chocolate pink with food colouring. Spread chocolate into 22cm x 30cm (8¾-inch x 12-inch) rectangle on tray; stand at room temperature about 5 minutes or until almost set. Cut 12 x 6.5cm (2¾-inch) hearts from chocolate (see page 230). Return to tray; refrigerate until set.

5 Meanwhile, freeze cake until firm. Slice cake into 12 x 1cm (½-inch) thick slices. Cut one 6.5cm (2¾-inch) heart from each slice.
6 Spread one side of all cakes with jam; top with chocolate hearts. Sandwich plain sides of cakes with ice-cream hearts. Serve immediately or return to freezer until required.

makes 6

coconut rough trio

100g (3 ounces) milk eating chocolate, melted
1½ cups (115g) toasted shredded coconut
100g (3 ounces) white eating chocolate, melted
100g (3 ounces) dark eating (semi-sweet) chocolate, melted

1 Grease 8cm x 26cm (3¼-inch x 10½-inch) bar pan; line with baking paper, extending paper 5cm (2 inches) over long sides.
2 Combine milk chocolate and ½ cup of the coconut in small bowl; spread mixture into pan. Refrigerate about 5 minutes or until firm.
3 Combine white chocolate and half of the remaining coconut in small bowl; spread mixture over milk chocolate base. Refrigerate about 5 minutes or until firm.
4 Combine dark chocolate and remaining coconut in small bowl; spread over white chocolate. Refrigerate about 30 minutes or until firm.
5 Remove from pan; stand 5 minutes before slicing with a hot, dry knife.

makes 25

sweet treats

In just one delicious mouthful, the
delicacies in this chapter will whisk you
away to a sugary paradise. Lovely lollies, the
most perfect, wobbling vanilla slice, exquisite
little bombes of fluffy sugar, soft, warm fudges
and delicate choux pastry – all to be eaten in
one breathtaking bite. These wonderful little
treasures are chic accompaniments
to serve with coffee or tea.

chocolate fudge

It is important to use a candy thermometer in this recipe (see page 247) to get the correct consistency when making the fudge.

1½ cups (330g) caster (superfine) sugar
½ cup (110g) firmly packed light brown sugar
60g (2 ounces) dark eating (semi-sweet) chocolate, chopped coarsely
2 tablespoons glucose syrup
½ cup (125ml) pouring cream
¼ cup (60ml) milk
40g (1½ ounces) unsalted butter, chopped

1 Grease deep 15cm (6-inch) square cake pan; line base with baking paper, extending paper 5cm (2 inches) over sides.
2 Combine sugars, chocolate, syrup, cream and milk in small heavy-based saucepan; stir over heat, without boiling, until sugar dissolves. Bring to the boil; boil, uncovered, without stirring, about 10 minutes or until syrup reaches 116°C/240°F on candy thermometer.
3 Remove pan from heat immediately, leave candy thermometer in the syrup; add butter, do not stir.
4 Cool fudge about 20 minutes or until the temperature of the syrup drops to 40°C/104°F; remove candy thermometer.
5 Stir fudge with wooden spoon about 10 minutes or until a small amount dropped from the spoon will hold its shape.
6 Quickly spread fudge into pan; cover with foil. Stand at room temperature about 3 hours or until fudge sets.
7 Lift fudge out of pan; cut into squares.

makes 49

minted chocolate creams

You need 25 foil petit four cases for this recipe.

100g (3 ounces) white eating chocolate, melted
2 tablespoons thickened (heavy) cream
200g (6½ ounces) dark eating (semi-sweet) chocolate, melted
peppermint oil or essence
green food colouring
¼ cup (35g) roasted unsalted pistachios, chopped finely

1 Combine white chocolate and cream in small bowl; refrigerate filling about 1 hour or until thickened, stirring occasionally.
2 Meanwhile, using small clean, dry artist's brush, brush dark chocolate inside 25 petit four cases (see page 232); place on tray, refrigerate until set.
3 Flavour filling with oil or essence to taste; tint with colouring.
4 Spoon filling into piping bag fitted with 5mm (¼-inch) fluted tube; pipe into chocolate cases. Carefully peel foil cases away from chocolate (see page 232); sprinkle filling with nuts.

makes 25

turkish delight

It is important to use a candy thermometer in this recipe (see page 247) in order to get the correct consistency required for turkish delight.

¼ cup (45g) gelatine
¼ cup (60ml) water
3 cups (660g) caster (superfine) sugar
2 cups (500ml) water, extra
¾ cup (110g) wheaten cornflour (cornstarch)
2 tablespoons glucose syrup
2½ tablespoons (50ml) rosewater essence
red food colouring
⅔ cup (110g) icing (confectioners') sugar, sifted

1 Grease deep 19cm (7¾-inch) square cake pan.
2 Sprinkle gelatine over the water in small jug; stand jug in small saucepan of simmering water. Stir until gelatine dissolves.
3 Combine caster sugar and ¾ cup of the extra water in medium saucepan; stir over heat, without boiling, until sugar dissolves. Bring to the boil; boil, without stirring, until temperature of the syrup reaches 116°C/240°F (soft ball) on candy thermometer. Simmer at 116°C/240°F for 5 minutes, without stirring, regulating heat to maintain temperature at 116°C/240°F. Remove pan from heat.
4 Meanwhile, place cornflour in another medium saucepan; gradually blend in the remaining extra water. Bring to the boil, stirring, until mixture boils and thickens.

5 Gradually stir hot sugar syrup, gelatine mixture and glucose into cornflour mixture; bring to the boil, stirring. Reduce heat; simmer, stirring, about 10 minutes or until mixture thickens a little more. Remove pan from heat; whisk in rosewater, tint with colouring.
6 Strain mixture through fine sieve into cake pan; skim any scum from surface. Stand 15 minutes; cover surface with lightly greased baking paper, stand overnight.
7 Turn turkish delight onto board dusted with icing sugar, dust with more icing sugar; cut with icing-sugar-coated-knife. Roll pieces in remaining icing sugar. Store turkish delight in an airtight container at room temperature for up to two weeks.

makes 48

You need 20 foil petit four cases for this recipe.

1 egg white
¼ cup (55g) caster (superfine) sugar
2 teaspoons caster (superfine) sugar, extra
1 tablespoon raspberry jam (conserve), warmed, sieved
2 teaspoons orange-flavoured liqueur
75g (2½ ounces) small strawberries, quartered

1 Preheat oven to 120°C/250°F. Place petit four cases on oven tray.
2 Beat egg white and 2 tablespoons of the sugar in small bowl with electric mixer until sugar is dissolved; fold in remaining 1 tablespoon sugar.
3 Drop rounded teaspoons of mixture into cases. Sprinkle meringues with extra sugar.
4 Bake about 25 minutes or until meringues are dry to touch. Cool meringues in oven with door ajar.
5 Meanwhile, combine jam and liqueur in small saucepan; stir over low heat until warm.
6 Gently press berries into top of each meringue; brush with warm jam mixture. Serve immediately.

makes 20

strawberry meringues

choc-mint slice

1 cup (220g) caster
   (superfine) sugar
⅔ cup (160ml) evaporated milk
2 teaspoons glucose syrup
15g (½ ounce) butter
100g (3 ounces) white
   marshmallows, chopped
400g (12½ ounces) dark eating
   (semi-sweet) chocolate,
   chopped coarsely
peppermint oil or essence

1 Grease 19cm x 29cm (7¾-inch x 11¾-inch) slice pan; line with baking paper, extending paper 5cm (2 inches) over long sides.
2 Combine sugar, milk, glucose and butter in medium heavy-based saucepan; stir over heat, without boiling, until sugar dissolves. Bring to the boil; boil, stirring, about 4 minutes or until mixture becomes the colour of creamed honey and begins to catch on the base of the pan.
3 Remove pan from heat; quickly stir in marshmallows and 250g (8 ounces) of the chocolate. Flavour mixture with oil or essence to taste (adding a few drops at a time). Spread mixture into pan.
4 Working quickly, melt remaining chocolate in small heatproof bowl over small saucepan of simmering water (see page 230); spread chocolate over slice. Refrigerate choc-mint slice until set before cutting.

makes 36

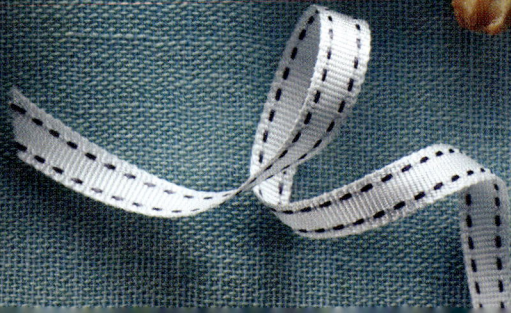

glazed almond biscuits

1 cup (120g) ground almonds
1 cup (160g) icing
   (confectioners') sugar
1 egg white
glaze
2 teaspoons gelatine
2 teaspoons caster
   (superfine) sugar
¼ cup (60ml) boiling water

1 Grease two oven trays; line with baking paper.
2 Combine ground almonds, sifted icing sugar and egg white in small bowl. Spoon mixture into piping bag fitted with 1cm (½-inch) fluted tube.
3 Pipe shapes onto trays. Stand, uncovered, overnight to dry.
4 Preheat oven to 200°C/400°F. Bake biscuits, uncovered, about 5 minutes or until browned lightly.
5 Meanwhile, make glaze.
6 Cool biscuits for 1 minute on trays; transfer to wire rack. Brush hot biscuits with hot glaze; cool.
glaze Combine ingredients in small jug; stir until sugar and gelatine dissolve.

makes 40

fruit mince slice

90g (3 ounces) butter, softened
⅓ cup (75g) firmly packed
   light brown sugar
1 cup (150g) plain
   (all-purpose) flour
topping
1 cup (340g) bottled fruit mince
2 eggs
½ cup (110g) firmly packed
   brown sugar
2 tablespoons brandy
1 tablespoon self-raising flour
1½ cups (120g) desiccated
   coconut

1 Preheat oven to 180°C/350°F. Grease 20cm x 30cm (8-inch x 12-inch) lamington pan; line with baking paper, extending paper 5cm (2 inches) over long sides.
2 Beat butter and sugar in small bowl with electric mixer until pale in colour; stir in sifted flour, in two batches. Press dough over base of pan. Bake 10 minutes.
3 Meanwhile, make topping.
4 Press topping gently over base. Bake about 25 minutes or until slice is firm and golden brown. Cool slice in pan before cutting.
topping Blend or process fruit mince until chopped finely. Beat eggs, sugar and brandy in small bowl with electric mixer until thick and creamy; fold in flour, coconut and mince.

makes 60

choccy orange sticks

2 large thick-skinned
    oranges (600g)
1 cup (220g) caster
    (superfine) sugar
1 cup (250ml) water
200g (6½ ounces) dark eating
    (semi-sweet) chocolate, melted

1 Cut oranges into quarters. Peel away skin, leaving pith attached to skin. Cut skin with pith into 1cm (½-inch) thick strips; discard fruit.
2 Drop orange strips into pan of boiling water, return to the boil; drain. Repeat twice.
3 Combine sugar and the water in medium saucepan. Stir over heat, without boiling, until sugar dissolves. Add strips; bring to the boil. Reduce heat; simmer, uncovered, stirring occasionally, about 5 minutes or until strips become translucent.
4 Meanwhile, place wire rack over baking-paper-lined tray.
5 Remove strips from syrup with tongs; place on wire rack in single layer. Dry, uncovered, overnight.
6 Line tray with baking paper. Using dipping forks (see page 232), dip strips, one at a time, into chocolate; place on tray. Set at room temperature.

makes 48

chocolate marzipan almonds

30 (40g) whole blanched
   almonds
200g (6½ ounces) marzipan or
   almond paste
125g (4 ounces) dark eating
   (semi-sweet) chocolate,
   melted

1 Preheat oven to 180°C/350°F.
2 Roast nuts in single layer on
oven tray about 5 minutes or
until golden brown; cool.
3 Mould level teaspoons of
paste around each nut. Place
on wire rack; stand, uncovered,
overnight, until dry to touch.
4 Using dipping forks, dip each
nut into chocolate (see page
232). Place nuts on foil-lined tray;
set at room temperature.

makes 30

cherry jubilee jellies

2 tablespoons gelatine
¾ cup (180ml) water
2 cups (440g) caster
  (superfine) sugar
¾ cup (180ml) water, extra
2 tablespoons cherry brandy

1 Sprinkle gelatine over the water in small jug; stand about 5 minutes or until softened.
2 Meanwhile, combine sugar and the extra water in medium saucepan; stir over heat, without boiling, until sugar dissolves. Reduce heat; simmer, uncovered, about 10 minutes or until syrup is thicker, but still clear. Add gelatine mixture, stir until dissolved, then stir in brandy. Stand 10 minutes; skim any scum from surface.
3 Pour mixture into wetted 8cm x 26cm (3¼-inch x 10½-inch) bar cake pan; refrigerate jelly about 3 hours or until firm.
4 Turn jelly onto board; cut into squares with hot, wet knife.

makes 52

jammy spice drops

30g (1 ounce) butter
⅓ cup (115g) golden syrup
1 cup (150g) plain
   (all-purpose) flour
½ teaspoon bicarbonate of
   (baking) soda
¼ teaspoon ground ginger
¼ teaspoon ground cardamom
¼ teaspoon ground cinnamon
¼ teaspoon ground cloves
½ teaspoon cocoa powder
1 tablespoon milk
2 tablespoons finely chopped
   mixed peel
¼ cup (80g) raspberry jam
   (conserve)
60g (2 ounces) dark eating
   (semi-sweet) chocolate,
   melted

1 Melt butter in small saucepan; add syrup, bring to the boil. Remove pan from heat; stand 10 minutes.
2 Stir in sifted dry ingredients, milk and peel. Cover; cool 2 hours.
3 Preheat oven to 180°C/350°F. Grease two oven trays.
4 Knead dough on surface dusted with a little extra flour until dough loses stickiness.
5 Roll dough between sheets of baking paper to about 8mm (½-inch) thickness. Cut out rounds using 4cm (1½-inch) fluted round cutter. Place about 3cm (1¼ inches) apart on trays.
6 Using end of handle of wooden spoon, gently press hollows into each round; fill with ½ teaspoon jam.
7 Bake 10 minutes; cool on trays.
8 Spread flat-sides of biscuits with chocolate. Place biscuits, jam-side down, on foil-lined trays; set at room temperature.

makes 24

lemon coconut macaroons

You can use a 300ml carton of cream in this recipe.

3 egg whites
2 tablespoons caster (superfine) sugar
1¼ cups (200g) icing (confectioners') sugar
½ cup (60g) ground almonds
½ cup (40g) desiccated coconut
1 tablespoon icing (confectioners') sugar, extra

lemon cream
1¼ cups (310ml) thickened (heavy) cream
1 tablespoon icing (confectioners') sugar
1 teaspoon finely grated lemon rind

1 Preheat oven to 150°C/300°F. Grease four oven trays; line with baking paper.
2 Beat egg whites in small bowl with electric mixer until soft peaks form. Add caster sugar; beat until sugar dissolves. Transfer mixture to large bowl. Fold in sifted icing sugar, ground almonds and coconut, in two batches.
3 Spoon mixture into large piping bag fitted with 1.5cm (¾-inch) plain tube. Pipe 4cm (1½-inch) rounds, about 2cm (¾ inch) apart, onto trays.
4 Tap trays on bench to help macaroons spread slightly. Dust macaroons with extra sifted icing sugar; stand 15 minutes.
5 Meanwhile, make lemon cream.
6 Bake macaroons 20 minutes. Stand 5 minutes; transfer to wire rack to cool.
7 Sandwich macaroons with lemon cream just before serving.
lemon cream Beat cream, icing sugar and rind in small bowl with electric mixer until firm peaks form.

makes 24

cherry almond coconut slice

60g (2 ounces) butter, softened
⅓ cup (75g) caster
   (superfine) sugar
1 egg yolk
2 tablespoons self-raising flour
½ cup (75g) plain
   (all-purpose) flour
⅔ cup (220g) cherry jam
   (conserve)
1 tablespoon cherry brandy
⅓ cup (25g) flaked almonds

topping

2 eggs
¼ cup (55g) caster
   (superfine) sugar
2 cups (160g) desiccated
   coconut

1 Preheat oven to 180°C/350°F. Grease 19cm x 29cm (7¾-inch x 11¾-inch) slice pan; line with baking paper, extending paper 5cm (2 inches) over long sides.
2 Beat butter, sugar and egg yolk in small bowl with electric mixer until light and fluffy. Stir in sifted flours. Press mixture into pan; spread with combined jam and brandy.
3 Make topping.
4 Sprinkle topping over slice, then sprinkle topping with nuts; press down gently.
5 Bake about 30 minutes; cool in pan before cutting.
topping Beat eggs and sugar together with fork in medium bowl; stir in coconut.

makes 54

sugary cinnamon twists

1 sheet puff pastry, thawed
20g (¾ ounce) butter, melted
2 tablespoons raw sugar
½ teaspoon ground cinnamon

1 Preheat oven to 200°C/400°F. Grease two oven trays.
2 Brush pastry with butter; sprinkle with combined sugar and cinnamon. Cut pastry in half. Turn one half over, sugar-side down; place the other half, sugar-side up, on top. Press lightly to join layers. Cut pastry into 1cm (½-inch) wide strips; twist each strip (see page 235), then place on trays.
3 Bake about 10 minutes or until browned lightly and crisp; transfer to wire rack to cool.

makes 25

If you would like to make your own delicious pastry cases, see the recipe for pastry in blueberry apple crumbles on page 217.

395g (12½ ounces) canned
   sweetened condensed milk
2 tablespoons golden syrup
60g (2 ounces) unsalted butter
24 x 4.5cm (1¾-inch) diameter
   baked pastry cases
1 large banana (230g)
½ cup (125ml) thickened (heavy)
   cream, whipped

1 Combine condensed milk, syrup and butter in small heavy-based saucepan; stir over heat until smooth.
2 Bring mixture to the boil; boil, stirring, about 10 minutes or until mixture is thick and dark caramel in colour. Remove pan from heat; cool.
3 Fill pastry cases with caramel; top with a slice of banana, then a dollop of cream.

makes 24

banoffee tartlets

apple charlotte tartlets

If you would like to make your own delicious pastry cases, see the recipe for pastry in blueberry apple crumbles on page 217.

2 medium green apples (300g), peeled, cored
1 tablespoon caster (superfine) sugar
1 tablespoon water
1 clove
½ teaspoon ground cinnamon
24 x 4.5cm (1¾-inch) diameter baked pastry cases
½ cup (125ml) thickened (heavy) cream, whipped
2 tablespoons passionfruit pulp

1 Thinly slice apples; combine in small saucepan with sugar, the water, clove and cinnamon; cover. Bring to the boil; reduce heat, simmer, covered, about 5 minutes or until apple softens.
2 Drain apple mixture; discard liquid and clove. Cool apple.
3 Place pastry cases on tray, fill with cold stewed apple; refrigerate 30 minutes.
4 Just before serving, top with cream, then drizzle with passionfruit pulp.

makes 24

If you would like to make your own delicious pastry cases, see the recipe for pastry in blueberry apple crumbles on page 217.

4 egg yolks
⅓ cup (75g) caster (superfine) sugar
2 teaspoons finely grated lemon rind
¼ cup (60ml) lemon juice
40g (1½ ounces) unsalted butter, chopped
24 x 4.5cm (1¾-inch) diameter baked pastry cases

meringue
1 egg white
¼ cup (55g) caster (superfine) sugar

1 Combine egg yolks, sugar, rind, juice and butter in small heatproof bowl; stir over small saucepan of simmering water until mixture thickens slightly and coats the back of a spoon. Remove pan from heat, remove bowl from pan immediately; cover surface of lemon curd with plastic wrap; refrigerate until cold.
2 Preheat oven to 200°C/400°F.
3 Meanwhile, make meringue.
4 Place pastry cases on oven tray; fill with curd, then top with meringue.
5 Bake about 5 minutes or until meringue is browned lightly.
meringue Beat egg white in small bowl with electric mixer until soft peaks form; gradually add sugar, beating until dissolved between additions.

makes 24

lemon meringue tartlets

creamy caramels

1 cup (220g) caster
   (superfine) sugar
90g (3 ounces) unsalted butter
2 tablespoons golden syrup
⅓ cup (115g) glucose syrup
½ cup (125ml) sweetened
   condensed milk

1 Grease deep 19cm (7¾-inch) square cake pan.
2 Combine sugar, butter, syrups, and milk in medium heavy-based saucepan; stir over heat, without boiling, until sugar is dissolved.
3 Bring to the boil; boil, stirring, about 7 minutes or until mixture is a caramel colour. Allow bubbles to subside; pour into pan, stand 10 minutes.
4 Mark squares using greased metal spatula (see page 237). Cool before cutting.

makes 81

anzac bites

½ cup (45g) rolled oats
60g (2 ounces) butter
1 tablespoon golden syrup
¼ teaspoon bicarbonate of
  (baking) soda
½ cup (75g) plain (all-purpose)
  flour
½ cup (110g) caster (superfine)
  sugar
⅓ cup (25g) desiccated coconut

1 Preheat oven to 150°C/300°F.
Grease two oven trays.
2 Blend or process oats until
chopped coarsely.
3 Combine butter and syrup in
medium saucepan; stir over low
heat until smooth. Remove pan
from heat; stir in soda, then
remaining ingredients.
4 Roll rounded teaspoons of the
mixture into balls. Place about
5cm (2 inches) apart on trays;
flatten slightly. Bake about
15 minutes; cool on trays.

makes 36

coconut ice

5¼ cups (840g) icing
  (confectioners') sugar
2½ cups (200g) desiccated
  coconut
395g (12½ ounces) canned
  sweetened condensed milk
1 egg white, beaten lightly
pink food colouring

1 Line deep 19cm (7¾-inch) square cake pan with strips of baking paper.
2 Sift icing sugar into large bowl; stir in coconut, then condensed milk and egg white.
3 Divide mixture in half; tint half with pink colouring. Press pink mixture into pan then top with white mixture. Cover; refrigerate about 3 hours or until set before cutting into squares.

makes 64

lime and berry friands

3 egg whites

90g (3 ounces) unsalted butter, melted

1 teaspoon finely grated lime rind

½ cup (60g) ground almonds

¾ cup (120g) icing (confectioners') sugar

¼ cup (35g) plain (all-purpose) flour

⅓ cup (50g) frozen blueberries

1 tablespoon icing (confectioners') sugar, extra

1 Preheat oven to 180°C/350°F. Grease two 12-hole (1-tablespoon/20ml) mini muffin pans.

2 Place egg whites in medium bowl, whisk until frothy. Stir in butter, rind, ground almonds and sifted icing sugar and flour.

3 Drop heaped teaspoons of mixture into each muffin pan hole; top each with a blueberry.

4 Bake about 10 minutes. Stand friands in pans 5 minutes; turn onto wire rack to cool.

5 Dust with sifted extra icing sugar.

makes 24

brandy snaps with hazelnut cream

This recipe makes a lot of tiny baskets; make as many as you need, then make the remaining mixture into larger snaps – serve them stacked, layered with cream, for an easy dessert.

1 tablespoon golden syrup
30g (1 ounce) butter
1½ tablespoons light
  brown sugar
1½ tablespoons plain
  (all-purpose) flour
1 teaspoon ground ginger
45 (⅓ cup) roasted hazelnuts
hazelnut cream
¾ cup (180ml) thickened
  (heavy) cream
1 tablespoon hazelnut-flavoured
  liqueur

1 Preheat oven to 180°C/350°F. Grease two oven trays.
2 Combine syrup, butter and sugar in small saucepan; stir over low heat until smooth. Remove pan from heat; stir in sifted flour and ginger.
3 Drop four level ¼-teaspoons of mixture, about 5cm (2 inches) apart, on oven tray (for easier handling, bake only four at a time).
4 Bake about 4 minutes or until golden brown. Remove from oven; cool on tray 30 seconds. With rounded knife or metal spatula, quickly lift brandy snap from tray (see page 241); shape each brandy snap into a basket-shape using an upturned foil petit-four case as a guide (see page 241). Repeat with remaining mixture.
5 Make hazelnut cream.
6 Just before serving, fill baskets with hazelnut cream; top each with a nut.
hazelnut cream Beat cream and liqueur in small bowl with electric mixer until firm peaks form.

makes 45

choc-topped zucottos

2 eggs
⅓ cup (75g) caster (superfine) sugar
2 tablespoons cornflour (cornstarch)
2 tablespoons plain (all-purpose) flour
2 tablespoons self-raising flour
200g (6½ ounces) milk eating chocolate
2 tablespoons icing (confectioners') sugar

nutty cream
½ cup (125ml) thickened (heavy) cream
1 tablespoon icing (confectioners') sugar
1 tablespoon hazelnut-flavoured liqueur
2 tablespoons finely chopped roasted hazelnuts
2 tablespoons finely chopped roasted almonds

1 Preheat oven to 180°C/350°F. Grease and flour three 12-hole shallow round-based patty pans (see page 247).
2 Beat eggs in small bowl with electric mixer until thick and creamy. Gradually add caster sugar, beating until sugar dissolves between additions. Sift flours together three times; fold into egg mixture.
3 Drop rounded tablespoons of mixture into pans. Bake about 7 minutes; turn onto wire racks to cool.
4 Meanwhile, coarsely grate 1 tablespoon of chocolate from the 200g (6½-ounce) block; reserve grated chocolate. Melt remaining chocolate (see page 230).
5 Make nutty cream.

6 Dip the knuckle of your index finger into icing sugar then use to make a large hollow in the flat side of the cakes (see page 239).
7 Spoon 1 teaspoon of the nutty cream into each hollow; smooth level. Spread with melted chocolate. Set at room temperature.
8 Dust zucottos with sifted icing sugar to serve.
nutty cream Beat cream, sifted icing sugar and liqueur in small bowl with electric mixer until firm peaks form. Stir in nuts and reserved grated chocolate.

makes 36

1 egg white
⅓ cup (55g) icing
   (confectioners') sugar
½ teaspoon vanilla extract
30g (1 ounce) butter, melted
¼ cup (30g) ground almonds
¼ cup (35g) plain
   (all-purpose) flour
filling
⅓ cup (50g) finely
   chopped raisins
¼ cup (60ml) dark rum
1 cinnamon stick
1 cup (240g) ricotta cheese
2 tablespoons honey

1 Preheat oven to 200°C/400°F. Grease two oven trays. Mark two 6cm (2½-inch) circles on each tray.
2 Beat egg white, sifted icing sugar and extract in small bowl with fork until foamy. Beat in butter, ground almonds and sifted flour.
3 Drop level teaspoons of mixture into circles, spread to fill circles. Bake about 4 minutes or until edges of cornettes are browned lightly (bake two cornettes at a time; they must be shaped quickly).
4 Using metal spatula, quickly lift one cornette from tray, roll into cone shape; hold gently until crisp (see page 239). Repeat with remaining mixture.

5 Make filling.
6 Spoon filling into piping bag fitted with 1cm (½-inch) plain tube. Pipe mixture into cornettes.
filling Combine raisins, rum and cinnamon in small saucepan, stir over low heat until warm; cool then discard cinnamon. Combine cheese and honey in small bowl; stir in raisin mixture.

makes 20

rum and raisin cornettes

jewelettes

½ cup (70g) roasted
   unsalted pistachios
¼ cup (50g) halved green
   glacé cherries
¼ cup (50g) halved red
   glacé cherries
¼ cup (60g) coarsely chopped
   glacé peaches
¼ cup (55g) coarsely chopped
   glacé ginger
200g (6½ ounces) white eating
   chocolate, melted

1 Grease 8cm x 26cm (3¼-inch x 10½-inch) bar cake pan; line base with baking paper, extending paper 5cm (2 inches) over long sides.
2 Combine nuts, fruits and ginger in medium bowl. Working quickly, stir in chocolate; spread mixture into pan, push down firmly to flatten. Refrigerate until set.
3 Turn bar onto board, cut into slices.

makes 16

pistachio almond crisps

3 egg whites
½ cup (110g) caster
   (superfine) sugar
pinch ground cardamom
1 cup (150g) plain
   (all-purpose) flour
½ cup (80g) blanched almonds
½ cup (70g) roasted unsalted
   pistachios

1 Preheat oven to 160°C/325°F. Grease 30cm (12-inch) square piece of foil.
2 Beat egg whites in small bowl with electric mixer until soft peaks form. Gradually add sugar, beating until dissolved between additions. Transfer mixture to medium bowl.
3 Fold in sifted dry ingredients and nuts; spoon mixture onto foil, shape into 7cm x 25cm (2¾-inch x 10-inch) log. Enclose firmly in foil; place on oven tray.
4 Bake about 45 minutes or until firm. Turn log out of foil onto wire rack to cool.
5 Preheat oven to 120°C/250°F.
6 Using serrated knife, slice log thinly. Place slices close together in single layer on oven trays. Bake about 20 minutes or until crisp; transfer to wire racks to cool. Store in airtight container at room temperature for up to four weeks.

makes 65

coconut ice-cream truffles

1 cup (250ml) vanilla ice-cream
2 teaspoons coconut-flavoured
   liqueur
1 tablespoon shredded coconut
125g (4 ounces) plain sweet
   biscuits, crushed
400g (12½ ounces) white eating
   chocolate, melted
1¾ cups (135g) shredded
   coconut, extra

1 Combine slightly softened ice-cream, liqueur, coconut and biscuit in medium bowl. Cover with foil; freeze about 1 hour or until firm.
2 Working quickly, roll ½ level teaspoons of mixture into balls. Place on tray; freeze until firm.
3 Dip balls in melted chocolate (see page 232); roll in extra coconut. Return to tray; freeze until firm.

makes 50

variations

hazelnut Replace liqueur with 1 tablespoon chocolate hazelnut spread. Omit shredded coconut. Replace white chocolate with milk chocolate. Replace extra shredded coconut with 1½ cups finely chopped roasted hazelnuts.
mocha walnut Replace liqueur with 1 tablespoon strong black coffee. Omit shredded coconut. Replace white chocolate with dark chocolate. Replace extra shredded coconut with 1½ cups finely chopped roasted walnuts.

Coconut ice-cream truffles and mocha walnut ice-cream truffles

almond honey nougat

It is important to use a candy thermometer in this recipe (see page 247) in order to get the correct consistency when making the nougat. Rice paper, used for confectionery, can be found in specialist food stores and some delicatessens.

2 sheets rice paper
½ cup (180g) honey
1⅓ cups (290g) caster (superfine) sugar
2 tablespoons water
1 egg white
2 cups (320g) blanched almonds, roasted

1 Grease deep 15cm (6-inch) square cake pan. Trim one sheet of rice paper to fit base of pan.
2 Combine honey, sugar and the water in small heavy-based saucepan with pouring lip; stir over heat, without boiling, until sugar dissolves. Bring to the boil; boil, without stirring, about 10 minutes or until syrup reaches 164°C/325°F on the candy thermometer; remove pan from heat immediately. Remove thermometer from pan.
3 Beat egg white in small heatproof bowl with electric mixer until soft peaks form. With motor operating, add hot syrup to egg white in thin, steady stream.

4 Stir nuts into egg white mixture; spoon into pan. Press mixture firmly into pan. Cut remaining sheet of rice paper large enough to cover top of nougat; press gently onto nougat. Stand at room temperature about 2 hours or until cool.
5 Cut nougat into squares. Store in airtight container at room temperature.

makes 49

rosewater pistachio crêpes

½ cup (75g) plain
  (all-purpose) flour
1 tablespoon caster
  (superfine) sugar
2 eggs
¾ cup (180ml) milk
1 tablespoon vegetable oil
¼ cup (35g) finely chopped
  roasted unsalted pistachios
rosewater cream
⅔ cup (160ml) thickened
  (heavy) cream
2 teaspoons icing
  (confectioners') sugar
½ teaspoon rosewater
pink food colouring

1 Sift flour and sugar into medium bowl, gradually stir in combined eggs, milk and oil; stir until smooth. Cover, stand 30 minutes.
2 Meanwhile, make rosewater cream.
3 Heat greased large heavy-based frying pan; pour ⅓ cup batter into pan, tilting pan to coat base evenly with batter.
4 Cook over low heat, loosening edge with spatula, until browned lightly. Turn crêpe; brown other side. Remove from pan. Repeat with remaining batter to make four crêpes. Using 6cm (2½-inch) fluted round cutter, cut eight rounds from each crêpe.

5 Spoon rosewater cream into piping bag fitted with 1cm (½-inch) plain tube. Pipe cream in centre of each round; pinch middle of crêpes together to join.
6 Dip ends of each filled crêpe into nuts.
rosewater cream Beat cream, icing sugar and rosewater in small bowl with electric mixer until firm peaks form; tint pink with colouring.

makes 32

PETITS

honey ginger crunchies

25g (¾ ounce) butter
1 tablespoon honey
1½ cups (60g) cornflakes
¼ cup (20g) flaked almonds,
  roasted
¼ cup (55g) finely chopped
  glacé ginger

1 Preheat oven to 180°C/350°F. Line two 12-hole (1-tablespoon/20ml) mini muffin pans with foil cases.
2 Melt butter with honey in small saucepan. Combine butter mixture with cornflakes, nuts and ginger in large bowl.
3 Drop level tablespoons of mixture into each case. Bake about 10 minutes or until golden. Cool in pans.

makes 24

This mixture will make 2 cups of mousse. Divide mousse among small glasses for serving – 40ml shot glasses will give you about 12 delicious mini servings.

30g (1 ounce) butter
120g (4 ounces) white eating chocolate
2 egg whites
⅔ cup (160ml) thickened (heavy) cream, whipped
green food colouring
2 teaspoons mint-flavoured liqueur

1 Melt butter in small saucepan or in microwave oven; stand 2 minutes. Skim off and reserve clarified butter from the top, leaving milky solids; discard solids.
2 Melt chocolate in medium heatproof bowl (see page 230); stir in clarified butter.
3 Beat egg whites in small bowl with electric mixer until soft peaks form. Gently fold egg white, cream and colouring into white chocolate mixture; stir in liqueur.
4 Divide mousse among serving glasses; refrigerate about 3 hours or overnight.
5 Decorate mousse with sliced strawberries and fresh mint leaves, if you like.

serves 12

minted white chocolate mousse

brandied cream cheese prunes

24 large prunes with seeds
1 tablespoon brandy
125g (4 ounces) cream cheese,
   softened
2 tablespoons icing
   (confectioners') sugar
1 tablespoon roasted flaked
   almonds, chopped coarsely
50g (1½ ounces) white eating
   chocolate, melted

1 Make a shallow cut lengthways in each prune (do not cut all the way through); remove seeds. Combine prunes and brandy in medium bowl; stand 15 minutes.
2 Meanwhile, combine cream cheese and sifted icing sugar in small bowl with wooden spoon; stir in nuts.
3 Drain brandy from prunes into cream cheese mixture; stir until combined. Place prunes on wire rack. Spoon cream cheese mixture into piping bag; pipe mixture into prunes (see page 239).
4 Drizzle prunes with melted chocolate (see page 230); set at room temperature.

makes 24

choc-orange ricotta dates

10 large fresh dates
1 tablespoon orange-flavoured
    liqueur
½ cup (120g) ricotta cheese
1 tablespoon icing
    (confectioners') sugar
1 teaspoon finely grated
    orange rind
50g (1½ ounces) dark eating
    (semi-sweet) chocolate,
    melted

1 Make a shallow cut lengthways in each date (do not cut all the way through); remove seeds. Combine dates and liqueur in medium bowl; stand 15 minutes.
2 Meanwhile, combine cheese, sifted icing sugar and rind in small bowl with wooden spoon.
3 Drain liqueur from dates into cream cheese mixture; stir until combined. Place dates on wire rack. Spoon cream cheese mixture into piping bag; pipe mixture into dates (see page 239).
4 Drizzle dates with melted chocolate (see page 230); set at room temperature.

makes 10

Store marshmallows in an airtight container at room temperature for up to two weeks.

2 tablespoons (28g) gelatine
½ cup (125ml) cold water
2 cups (440g) caster (superfine) sugar
1 cup (250ml) hot water
1 teaspoon rosewater
pink food colouring
1 cup (80g) desiccated coconut
¼ cup (20g) shredded coconut

1 Grease 25cm x 30cm (10-inch x 12-inch) swiss roll pan.
2 Sprinkle gelatine over the cold water in small bowl.
3 Combine sugar and the hot water in medium saucepan, stir over heat until sugar dissolves; bring to the boil. Add in gelatine mixture; boil, without stirring, 20 minutes. Cool to lukewarm.
4 Beat sugar mixture, flavouring and colouring in large bowl with electric mixer, on high speed, about 5 minutes or until mixture is thick and holds its shape.
5 Spread marshmallow mixture into swiss roll pan. Sprinkle marshmallow with a little of the combined coconut to cover top evenly. Set at room temperature for about 2 hours or until firm.
6 Cut marshmallow into squares.

makes 105

variations
orange Instead of the rosewater and pink food colouring, flavour the mixture with 1 teaspoon orange blossom water and tint with orange food colouring.
mint Instead of the rosewater and pink food colouring, flavour with ½ teaspoon peppermint essence or a few drops of peppermint oil and tint with green food colouring.

pink marshmallows

palmiers with honey cream

You can use a 300ml carton of cream in this recipe.

2 tablespoons raw sugar
1 sheet puff pastry
1 teaspoon ground nutmeg
1¼ cups (310ml) thickened (heavy) cream
2 teaspoons honey

1 Preheat oven to 180°C/350°F. Grease two oven trays; line with baking paper.
2 Sprinkle board lightly with a little of the sugar. Roll pastry on sugared board into 20cm x 40cm (8-inch x 16-inch) rectangle; trim edges. Sprinkle pastry with nutmeg and remaining sugar.
3 Starting from long side, loosely roll one side at a time into the middle of the rectangle, so the two long sides meet (see page 234).
4 Cut pastry into 5mm (¼-inch) thick pieces. Place, cut-side up, about 5cm (2 inches) apart, on trays. Spread pastry open slightly at folded ends to make a V-shape (see page 234).
5 Bake palmiers about 15 minutes or until golden brown; transfer to wire rack to cool.
6 Beat cream and honey in small bowl with electric mixer until firm peaks form. Serve palmiers with honey cream.

makes 30

lemon shortbread

We found the combination of regular table (salted) butter with unsalted butter gave the yummiest results.

60g (2 ounces) unsalted butter, softened
60g (2 ounces) butter, softened
2 teaspoons finely grated lemon rind
2 tablespoons caster (superfine) sugar
1 cup (150g) plain (all-purpose) flour
2 tablespoons rice flour
1 tablespoon demerara sugar

1 Preheat oven to 160°C/325°F. Grease two oven trays.
2 Beat butters, rind and caster sugar in small bowl with electric mixer until light and fluffy.
3 Stir in sifted flours in two batches. Turn dough onto floured surface, knead dough for 5 minutes.
4 Roll dough between sheets of baking paper until 5mm (¼-inch) thick. Using 5cm (2-inch) star-shaped cutter, cut out stars. Place about 3cm (1¼ inches) apart on trays.
5 Sprinkle stars with demerara sugar. Bake about 10 minutes; transfer to wire racks to cool.

makes 15

butteryscotch

2 cups (440g) caster
  (superfine) sugar
⅓ cup (80ml) water
⅔ cup (230g) glucose syrup
125g (4 ounces) unsalted butter,
  chopped

1 Grease 19cm x 29cm (7¾-inch x 11¾-inch) slice pan; line base with baking paper, extending paper 5cm (2 inches) over long sides.
2 Combine sugar, the water and glucose in medium heavy-based saucepan; stir over heat, without boiling, until sugar is dissolved. Bring to the boil; boil, uncovered, about 15 minutes or until mixture is golden brown (150°C/350°F on a candy thermometer, see page 247).
3 Remove pan from heat; allow bubbles to subside. Add butter; stir gently until smooth. Pour into slice pan; stand 10 minutes. Using greased metal spatula, mark butterscotch into squares (see page 237).
4 Cool butterscotch at room temperature. When cold, break into pieces.

makes 150

Weipa
Aurukun
Chicago
Tabriz
Urmia
Orkney Is.
Robe River
Deepdale
Mount Tom Pr
Paraburdoo
Bristol
Portsmouth
London
Corsica
Marseilles
Naples
ITALY
MOZAMBIQUE
Caroline Is.
(U.S.)
PHILIPPINES
TAIWAN

1½ cups (330g) caster
  (superfine) sugar
½ cup (125ml) water
2 teaspoons glucose syrup
15g (½ ounce) butter
1 tablespoon rum
¾ cup (120g) brazil nuts

1 Combine sugar, the water and glucose in large heavy-based saucepan; stir over heat, without boiling, until sugar is dissolved. Bring to the boil; boil about 20 minutes or until a teaspoon of hot toffee will set and crack when dropped into a cup of cold water.

2 Meanwhile, line oven trays with baking paper.

3 Remove pan from heat, allow bubbles to subside; add butter and rum, stir gently. Add nuts; tilt pan until nuts are well coated in toffee mixture.

4 Working quickly, using greased tongs or two forks, lift nuts, one at a time, out of toffee; place on tray, set at room temperature.

makes 40

buttered rum brazil nuts

lamingtonettes

We've used shredded coconut in our picture, but feel free to mix and match using shredded, desiccated or flaked. If you use flaked coconut, be sure to blend or process it until it's chopped coarsely; this helps it to stick to the icing.

90g (3 ounces) butter, softened
½ teaspoon vanilla extract
½ cup (110g) caster (superfine) sugar
2 eggs
1 cup (150g) self-raising flour
2 tablespoons milk
2¼ cups (180g) shredded coconut

chocolate icing
2 cups (320g) icing (confectioners') sugar
¼ cup (25g) cocoa powder
10g (½ ounce) butter
½ cup (125ml) milk

1 Preheat oven to 180°C/350°F. Grease 19cm x 29cm (7¾-inch x 11¾-inch) slice pan; line with baking paper.
2 Beat butter, extract, sugar, eggs, flour and milk in small bowl with electric mixer on low speed until ingredients are combined. Increase speed to medium; beat until mixture is pale in colour. Spread mixture evenly into pan.
3 Bake cake about 20 minutes. Stand 5 minutes; turn onto wire rack to cool. Cover with plastic wrap; stand overnight.
4 Trim top and sides from cake to make cake a 18cm x 28cm (7¼-inch x 11¼-inch) rectangle. Cut cake into 2cm (¾-inch) squares. Freeze squares about 30 minutes before dipping in icing.
5 Make chocolate icing.

6 Place coconut in small bowl. Hold each cake on a bamboo skewer, dip into icing; hold over bowl to drain excess icing.
7 Toss cakes, one at a time, in coconut. Stand lamingtonettes on wire rack until set.
chocolate icing Sift icing sugar and cocoa into medium heatproof bowl; stir in butter and milk. Stand bowl over hot water; stir until icing is of a good coating consistency. As icing thickens, add a little hot water to bring it back to the correct consistency.

makes 126

Katie dress

Amanda Tunic

and floral print chemise

cotton drawstring pant/capri

Katie top

Del Paige Top

Victorian cami

coffee meringue kisses

¾ cup (165g) caster (superfine) sugar
1 teaspoon instant coffee granules
¼ cup (60ml) water
1 egg white
1 teaspoon malt vinegar
2 teaspoons cornflour (cornstarch)

coffee butter cream

1 teaspoon instant coffee granules
2 teaspoons hot water
2 teaspoons coffee-flavoured liqueur
60g (2 ounces) unsalted butter, softened
⅔ cup (110g) icing (confectioners') sugar

1 Preheat oven to 120°C/250°F. Grease four oven trays; line with baking paper.
2 Combine sugar, coffee and the water in small saucepan; stir over heat until sugar is dissolved. Bring to the boil; remove pan from heat.
3 Meanwhile, combine egg white, vinegar and cornflour in small heatproof bowl; beat with electric mixer until foamy. With motor operating, add hot syrup to egg white in a thin, steady stream; beat about 10 minutes or until mixture is thick.

4 Spoon meringue into piping bag fitted with 5mm (¼-inch) fluted tube; pipe meringues, about 2.5cm (1 inch) in diameter, about 3cm (1¼ inches) apart, on trays. Bake about 30 minutes or until dry to touch. Cool on trays.
5 Meanwhile, make coffee butter cream. Sandwich meringues with butter cream just before serving.
coffee butter cream Dissolve coffee in the water; add liqueur. Beat butter and sifted icing sugar until light and fluffy; beat in coffee mixture.

makes 45

strawberry powder puffs

2 eggs
⅓ cup (75g) caster
   (superfine) sugar
2 tablespoons cornflour
   (cornstarch)
2 tablespoons plain
   (all-purpose) flour
2 tablespoons self-raising flour
½ cup (125ml) thickened
   (heavy) cream
2 tablespoons icing
   (confectioners') sugar
½ cup (65g) finely chopped
   strawberries

1 Preheat oven to 180°C/350°F. Grease and flour two 12-hole shallow round-based patty pans.
2 Beat eggs and sugar in small bowl with electric mixer about four minutes or until thick and creamy.
3 Meanwhile, triple-sift flours; fold into egg mixture.
4 Drop 1 teaspoon of mixture into holes of pans. Bake about 7 minutes; turn immediately onto wire racks to cool. Wash, grease and flour pans again; continue using mixture until all puffs are baked.
5 Beat cream and half the sifted icing sugar in small bowl with electric mixer until firm peaks form; fold in strawberries.
6 Sandwich puffs with strawberry cream just before serving. Dust with remaining sifted icing sugar.

makes 36

¼ cup (60ml) water
30g (1 ounce) butter
¼ cup (35g) plain
    (all-purpose) flour
1 egg, beaten lightly
1 tablespoon icing
    (confectioners') sugar
coffee liqueur cream
⅔ cup (160ml) thickened
    (heavy) cream
1 tablespoon icing
    (confectioners') sugar
1 tablespoon coffee-flavoured
    liqueur

1 Preheat oven to 200°C/400°F. Lightly grease two oven trays.
2 Combine the water and butter in small saucepan, bring to the boil; add sifted flour, stirring until mixture leaves side of pan. Remove pan from heat; cool 5 minutes.
3 Transfer mixture to small bowl; beat with electric mixer on medium speed. Gradually add egg, beating until mixture is glossy.
4 Spoon mixture into small piping bag fitted with 1.5cm (¾-inch) plain tube. Pipe 2cm (¾-inch) rounds, about 5cm (2 inches) apart, onto oven trays.
5 Bake 10 minutes. Reduce heat to 180°C/350°F; bake 20 minutes or until puffs are crisp.

6 Remove puffs from oven; make small slits in sides of each puff to let steam escape. Transfer puffs to wire rack to cool.
7 Meanwhile, make coffee liqueur cream.
8 Just before serving, place coffee liqueur cream in small piping bag fitted with 4mm (¼-inch) plain tube. Make small hole in bottom of each puff; pipe cream into puffs. Dust with sifted icing sugar.
coffee liqueur cream Beat cream, sifted icing sugar and liqueur in small bowl with electric mixer until firm peaks form.

makes 15

coffee liqueur puffs

little apricot macaroons

¼ cup (40g) finely chopped
   dried apricots
1 teaspoon orange-flavoured
   liqueur
1 egg white
¼ cup (55g) caster
   (superfine) sugar
1 cup (75g) desiccated coconut
1 tablespoon finely chopped
   white eating chocolate

1 Preheat oven to 150°C/300°F.
Line two 12-hole (1-tablespoon/
20ml) mini muffin pans with
paper cases.
2 Combine apricots and liqueur
in small bowl.
3 Beat egg whites in another small
bowl with electric mixer until soft
peaks form; gradually add sugar,
beating until dissolved between
additions. Fold in apricot mixture,
coconut and chocolate.
4 Place 1 heaped teaspoon in
each paper case. Bake about
20 minutes; cool in pans.

makes 24

sienna discs

2 tablespoons caster
   (superfine) sugar
¼ cup (90g) honey
⅓ cup (55g) blanched
   almonds, roasted
½ cup (70g) roasted hazelnuts
1 glacé apricot (30g)
1 glacé pineapple ring (30g)
2 tablespoons mixed peel
⅓ cup (50g) plain
   (all-purpose) flour
1 tablespoon cocoa powder
½ teaspoon ground cinnamon
30g (1 ounce) dark eating
   (semi-sweet) chocolate,
   melted
100g (3 ounces) dark eating
   (semi-sweet) chocolate,
   melted, extra

1 Preheat oven to 160°C/325°F.
Grease 40cm (16-inch) long
strip of foil.
2 Combine caster sugar and
honey in small saucepan; stir
over heat until sugar is dissolved.
Bring to a simmer; simmer,
without stirring, until syrup
thickens slightly. Remove pan
from heat.
3 Meanwhile, chop nuts, fruit and
peel finely; combine mixture in
medium bowl with syrup.
4 Stir in sifted flour, cocoa and
cinnamon, then chocolate.
5 Shape mixture into 5cm (2-inch)
diameter log; roll tightly in foil,
place on oven tray.
6 Bake 45 minutes; remove foil,
cool on tray overnight.
7 Slice log; place slices on wire
racks, pipe or drizzle extra
chocolate over slices (see page
233). Set at room temperature.

makes 30

peanut brittle pops

Using a saucepan with a pouring lip (see page 247) makes it easy to pour the hot toffee into the pan holes.

3 cups (660g) caster
   (superfine) sugar
1 cup (250ml) water
½ cup (70g) unsalted
   roasted peanuts
12 paddle-pop sticks

1 Stir sugar and the water in medium heavy-based saucepan over heat until sugar dissolves. Bring to the boil; boil about 10 minutes or until toffee turns golden brown (see page 236).
2 Remove pan from heat; allow bubbles to subside.
3 Meanwhile, divide nuts among two greased 12-hole (1-tablespoon/20ml) mini muffin pans. Cut paddle-pop sticks in half.
4 Pour toffee slowly over nuts; cool pops about 10 minutes. Position a paddle-pop stick, cut-side down, in each pop. Cool at room temperature.

makes 24

1 sheet puff pastry
¼ cup (55g) caster (superfine) sugar
¼ cup (35g) cornflour (cornstarch)
1½ tablespoons custard powder
1¼ cups (310ml) milk
30g (1 ounce) butter
1 egg yolk
½ teaspoon vanilla extract

passionfruit icing
¾ cup (110g) icing (confectioners') sugar
1 tablespoon passionfruit pulp
1 teaspoon water, approximately

1 Preheat oven to 240°C/475°F. Grease 8cm x 26cm (3¼-inch x 10½-inch) bar cake pan; line with strip of foil extending over long sides of pan.

2 Place pastry sheet on oven tray. Bake about 15 minutes or until puffed; cool. Split pastry in half horizontally; remove and discard any uncooked pastry from centre. Flatten pastry pieces gently with hand; trim both to fit pan. Place top half in pan, top-side down.

3 Meanwhile, combine sugar, cornflour and custard powder in medium saucepan; gradually stir in milk. Stir over heat until mixture boils and thickens. Reduce heat; simmer, stirring, about 3 minutes or until custard is thick and smooth. Remove pan from heat; stir in butter, egg yolk and extract.

4 Spread hot custard over the pastry in pan; top with remaining pastry, bottom-side up, press down gently. Cool to room temperature.

5 Meanwhile, make passionfruit icing.

6 Spread pastry with icing; set at room temperature. Refrigerate 3 hours before cutting.

passionfruit icing Sift icing sugar into small heatproof bowl; stir in passionfruit and enough water to make a thick paste. Stir over small saucepan of simmering water until icing is spreadable.

makes 8

vanilla passionfruit slice

lemon madeleines

2 eggs
2 tablespoons caster (superfine) sugar
2 tablespoons icing (confectioners') sugar
2 teaspoons finely grated lemon rind
¼ cup (35g) plain (all-purpose) flour
¼ cup (35g) self-raising flour
75g (2½ ounces) unsalted butter, melted
1 tablespoon lemon juice
2 tablespoons icing (confectioners') sugar, extra

1 Preheat oven to 200°C/400°F. Grease 12-hole (1½-tablespoon/ 30ml) madeleine tin (page 247).
2 Beat eggs, caster sugar, sifted icing sugar and rind in small bowl with electric mixer until pale and thick.
3 Meanwhile, triple-sift flours; sift flour over egg mixture. Pour butter and juice down the side of the bowl then fold ingredients together.
4 Drop rounded tablespoons of mixture into each hole of tin. Bake about 10 minutes. Tap hot tin firmly on bench to release madeleines onto wire rack to cool.
5 Dust with sifted extra icing sugar to serve.

makes 12

向上

blueberry apple crumbles

1 cup (150g) plain
  (all-purpose) flour
⅓ cup (55g) icing
  (confectioners') sugar
90g (3 ounces) unsalted
  butter, chopped
1 egg yolk
3 teaspoons iced water,
  approximately
2 tablespoons roasted
  slivered almonds
filling
1 small apple (130g),
  grated coarsely
½ cup (75g) frozen blueberries
1 teaspoon ground cinnamon
2 teaspoons finely grated
  lemon rind

1 Preheat oven to 180°C/350°F. Grease two 12-hole (1-tablespoon/20ml) mini muffin pans.
2 Pulse sifted flour, sugar and butter in food processor until crumbly. Add egg yolk and enough of the water to make mixture come together.
3 Shape one-quarter of the dough into thick sausage; wrap in plastic, freeze 45 minutes.
4 Meanwhile, roll remaining dough to 4mm (¼-inch) thickness, cut out 6cm (2½-inch) rounds (see page 235); press dough into holes of pan (see page 235). Refrigerate 15 minutes.
5 Make filling; divide filling into pastry cases.
6 Coarsely grate frozen dough evenly over filling; sprinkle with nuts. Bake about 20 minutes. Stand 5 minutes; transfer to wire rack to cool.
filling Combine apple, berries, cinnamon and rind in small bowl.

makes 24

bumble bee licorice

150g (4½ ounces) soft
    fondant icing
yellow food colouring
10 sticks soft licorice (125g)
½ cup (80g) icing
    (confectioners') sugar

1 Tint 100g (3 ounces) of the soft icing yellow by kneading food colouring into the icing on a surface dusted with sifted icing sugar. Knead remaining white icing until soft. Enclose icings separately in plastic wrap until ready to use.
2 Roll pieces of licorice firmly with rolling pin to about 3mm (⅛-inch) thick (see page 240).
3 Roll pieces of soft icing to the same thickness as licorice pieces (see page 240).
4 Stack the licorice and icing pieces, alternating colours (see page 240).
5 Cut stack into 2cm (¾-inch) pieces (see page 241). Stand pieces on baking-paper-lined tray until firm.

makes 20

toffeecomb with chocolate dip

It is important to use a candy thermometer in this recipe (see page 247) in order to get the correct consistency when making the toffee.

1 cup (220g) caster (superfine) sugar
¼ cup (90g) golden syrup
1 tablespoon water
1 tablespoon bicarbonate of (baking) soda
125g (4 ounces) dark eating (semi-sweet) chocolate, melted
2 tablespoons pouring cream

1 Grease 19cm x 29cm (7¾ inch x 11¾ inch) slice pan.
2 Combine sugar, syrup and the water in medium heavy-based saucepan; stir over heat, without boiling, until sugar dissolves.
3 Place candy thermometer in syrup, bring to the boil; boil 5 minutes or until temperature reaches 148°C/298°F.
4 Remove pan from heat; immediately stir in soda.
5 Using metal spatula, quickly spread mixture into pan; cool at room temperature.
6 Break toffeecomb into pieces. Serve with combined chocolate and cream.

serves 10

1 cup (150g) self-raising flour
1 tablespoon caster
   (superfine) sugar
1 egg
1¼ cups (310ml) buttermilk
25g (¾ ounce) unsalted butter,
   melted
½ cup (70g) fresh raspberries,
   chopped coarsely
½ cup (120g) crème fraîche
½ cup (70g) fresh raspberries,
   extra

1 Sift flour and sugar into medium bowl. Whisk egg, buttermilk and butter in medium jug.
2 Gradually whisk egg mixture into flour mixture until smooth. Stir in chopped raspberries. Transfer batter to jug.
3 Pour 1 tablespoon batter into heated greased large heavy-based frying pan for each pikelet. Cook pikelets until bubbles appear on the surface; turn each pikelet with metal spatula to brown lightly on the other side. Grease pan as needed during cooking. Cool pikelets on wire rack.
4 Serve pikelets topped with crème fraîche and extra raspberries.

makes 30

raspberry pikelets with crème fraîche

chocolate peanut butter flowers

180g (5½ ounces) white eating chocolate, chopped coarsely
1 tablespoon smooth peanut butter
200g (6½ ounces) dark eating (semi-sweet) chocolate, chopped coarsely

1 Grease 25cm x 30cm (10-inch x 12-inch) swiss roll pan; line base with baking paper, extending paper 5cm (2 inches) above long sides of pan.
2 Melt white chocolate in small heatproof bowl (see page 230); stir in peanut butter.
3 Melt dark chocolate in another small heatproof bowl; cool 5 minutes.
4 Drop alternate tablespoonfuls of white chocolate mixture and dark chocolate into pan.
5 Gently shake pan to level mixture; pull a skewer backwards and forwards through mixture several times for a marbled effect. Stand at room temperature about 2 hours or until set.
6 Using 5cm (2 inches) flower cutter, cut out shapes; store in single layer in refrigerator.

makes 28

15 medium strawberries
1 tablespoon liqueur of your
   choice, approximately
⅓ cup (80ml) double cream

1 Cut small slice from pointy end of each strawberry so they stand upright. Cut tops off strawberries.
2 Using small pointed knife, hollow out strawberry centres.
3 Pour about ¼ teaspoon of liqueur into each strawberry.
4 Using teaspoon or small piping bag fitted with 1.5cm (¾-inch) plain tube, pipe cream into strawberries. Position strawberry tops on cream.

makes 15

strawberry liqueur surprises

tips & techniques

Melting chocolate

Place chocolate in a small heatproof bowl over a small saucepan of simmering water. Do not allow the water to touch the bottom of the bowl. Stir the chocolate until smooth, then immediately remove the bowl from the pan. Do not allow any water to come in contact with the chocolate or it will seize.

Making chocolate curls

Spread melted chocolate evenly over a cold surface, such as marble or a flat oven tray; leave at room temperature until almost set. Drag the blade of a large sharp knife, held at about a 45° angle, across the chocolate, to make curls. It is important that chocolate is at the right stage. If chocolate is not set enough, it will not curl and if the chocolate is set too much the curls will break. Another way to make simple chocolate curls is to scrape along the side of a block of chocolate with a vegetable peeler.

Cutting hearts from coloured chocolate

Spread chocolate evenly onto baking-paper-lined tray and leave at room temperature until almost set. Carefully cut 12 x 6.5cm (2¾-inch) hearts from chocolate; refrigerate until chocolate is set.

Wrapping frozen chocolate tiramisu bars in chocolate

Trace a 12cm x 15cm (4¾-inch x 6-inch) rectangle on a piece of paper to use as a guide. Place a sheet of plastic wrap over paper. Spread chocolate over plastic wrap, into rectangle shape, using guide. Working quickly, place one ice-cream bar in centre of chocolate rectangle; lift corners and sides of plastic wrap above ice-cream bar to encase bottom and sides in chocolate. Place on a tray and freeze until chocolate sets.

Unwrapping frozen chocolate tiramisu bars

Once the chocolate has set, working with one bar at a time (keep remaining bars in freezer), carefully peel the plastic wrap away from the chocolate. Serve tiramisu bars immediately dusted with sifted cocoa powder or return to freezer until required.

Assembling black forest chocolate boxes

Spread chocolate onto baking-paper-lined tray into a 32cm (12¾-inch) square and allow to set at room temperature. Trim chocolate to a 30cm (12-inch) square, then cut square into 36 x 5cm (2-inch) squares. Cut each square in half to give 72 x 2.5cm x 5cm (1-inch x 2-inch) rectangles. Spread the sides of each cake with a little warmed and sieved jam. Carefully press chocolate rectangles onto sides of cakes, ensuring all corners are aligned, to create chocolate boxes.

Dipping in chocolate

Allow melted chocolate to cool slightly until it is a good coating consistency. Using two forks, or even better dipping forks (see page 247), dip truffles or almonds in and out of the chocolate; drain off excess chocolate, then place on a baking-paper-lined tray and refrigerate until chocolate is set. For ice-cream truffles, ensure truffles are frozen solid before you start dipping and work with a few truffles at a time (keep the rest in the freezer); roll in coating and freeze until firm.

Painting petit four cases & easter egg moulds with chocolate

Use small foil petit four cases as they are quite strong and rigid enough to handle the chocolate; use clean, dry plastic easter egg moulds (see page 245). Foil cases and moulds are available from specialty cookware shops. Use an artist's brush (see page 247) dipped in melted chocolate to brush a thick layer of chocolate evenly inside each foil case and mould. Cases and moulds are best left to set at room temperature; if you're in a hurry, refrigerate them.

Removing petit four cases & easter egg moulds

Once chocolate cases have set, using your fingers, and handling the cases gently, ease the foil cases away from the chocolate; you'll be surprised how easy it is. If the cases are refrigerator-cold, leave them to stand for about 10 minutes to reach room temperature, before removing the foil cases. To remove eggs from moulds, carefully invert mould onto board and gently tap eggs with finger until the eggs release from the mould.

Piping chocolate

Use a plastic or fabric piping bag (see page 238) fitted with a fine plain piping tube, or a paper piping bag made from baking paper (see page 238). Half-fill the bag with melted chocolate. Use sharp scissors to snip a tiny piece from the tip of the paper bag to pipe through. If the hole is too small, continue to snip tiny pieces off until you can pipe the right thickness of chocolate.

Piping mocha cream hearts

Trace eight 7cm (2¾-inch) hearts on a piece of baking paper; place on a greased oven tray. Spoon the choux mixture into a piping bag fitted with a 5mm (¼-inch) plain tube. Pipe half of the mixture onto paper, tracing outlines of hearts, then filling centres. Pipe the remaining mixture directly on top of the first hearts. You will have eight double-layered hearts. Bake hearts until crisp, then carefully split in half, horizontally, using a serrated knife. Return to oven to dry out.

Assembling mocha cream hearts

Place tops of hearts on a wire rack over a tray and spread with the melted chocolate; leave to set at room temperature. Fill the bases of hearts with the mocha cream, then top with chocolate coated hearts.

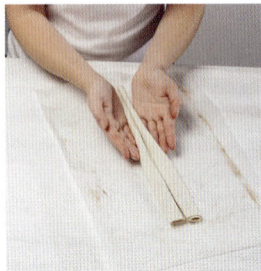

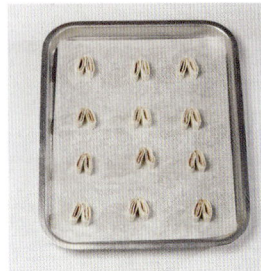

Folding pastry for palmiers

Roll the sheet of thawed puff pastry on a sugared surface to 20cm x 40cm (8 inches x 16 inches). Using a sharp knife, trim all four sides neatly, keeping the rectangular shape. Sprinkle the pastry evenly with sugar and nutmeg. Starting from a long side, loosely roll one side at a time into the middle of the rectangle, so the two long sides meet.

Fold the long outside edges into the centre again. Turn the pastry piece on its side.

Preparing palmiers for baking

Use a sharp knife to cut each palmier about 5cm (2 inches) in thickness; put them, cut-side up, on a baking-paper-lined oven tray, about 5cm (2 inches) apart. Gently pull the pastry apart to make a V-shape, this will help shape the palmiers during baking.

Shaping sugary cinnamon twists

Gently twist each strip of pastry by holding ends of each strip with fingers, and turning each end in a different direction; place twists about 5cm (2 inches) apart on baking-paper-lined oven trays.

Handling pastry

Divide pastry in half, or quarters, depending on how much pastry you can handle at the one time, this pastry is quite soft. Roll chilled pastry between sheets of baking paper to 4mm (¼-inch) thickness. Using sharp 6cm (2½-inch) cutter, cut out rounds from pastry.

Lining pans with pastry

Gently ease each round of pastry into each hole of the muffin pan; don't stretch the pastry. You'll get an even better result with this pastry if you refrigerate it for about 30 minutes before baking. This will help reduce shrinkage of the pastry and result in crisper pastry cases.

Handling sugar syrup

Use a heavy-based saucepan of the size we suggest, so that the correct amount of evaporation can take place. We indicate cooking times in our recipes, but they're only a guide. Stir the sugar and water over a medium to high heat until the sugar is dissolved, remove any sugar crystals on the side of the pan with a brush dipped in water.

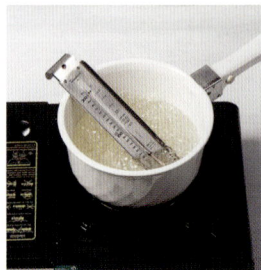

Using a candy thermometer

The correct way to use a thermometer is to place it in a small saucepan of cold water, bring it to the boil, check for accuracy then, when the syrup is boiling, transfer the thermometer into the syrup. After the correct temperature is reached, return the thermometer to the pan of boiling water, turn off the heat, and leave the thermometer to cool with the water.

Boiling sugar syrup

If we suggest you use a candy thermometer, the temperature of the syrup will be critical for success. But, with basic toffees and caramels, you can easily get away with testing the syrup/toffee in water. After some practice, you'll recognise the colour that the sugar syrup should be.

Testing toffee or caramel

When you think the syrup has reached the colour we suggest, remove the pan from the heat, remembering that the syrup will continue to cook and darken during this time, so allow for this. Let the bubbles subside, then drop a teaspoon of the syrup into a cup of cold water.

Judging toffee

The toffee will set the instant it hits the cold water; lift it out and break it with your fingers. Taste a piece and, if you decide after this that the toffee needs to be a richer caramel flavour, or harder, then return the mixture to the heat and cook a little more. This test is easy, but a thermometer removes all the guess work for you.

Marking caramel/ butterscotch

If you want a caramel to be cut into neat pieces, then it's vital that you mark the unset mixture before it sets. The right time to mark the caramel varies depending on the temperature reached. Grease the blade of a thin metal spatula or large knife, and, after the caramel has stood about 10 minutes, start to mark a line in the caramel. If the line doesn't hold its shape, then wait a few more minutes. Mark the caramel all the way through to the base of the pan.

Making a paper piping bag

Cut a 25cm (10-inch) square from a sheet of baking or greaseproof paper; fold the square in half diagonally then cut out the two triangles. With the apex of one triangle pointing towards you, hold the other two points, wrapping them around to form a cone.

Bring the three points of the triangle together. Secure the bag with a staple if you're using baking paper, or with sticky tape if you're using greaseproof paper. Half-fill the bag with icing etc, then, using sharp scissors, snip a tiny piece from the point of the bag for piping.

Ready-made piping bags

There are many types, shapes and sizes available. Rolls of plastic disposable piping bags are available from supermarkets, complete with various-shaped plastic piping tubes. Bags made from various types of fabrics are available from specialty cookware shops, and cake-decorator supplier shops.

Shaping zucottos

As soon as the baked zucottos are cool enough to handle, use the knuckle of your forefinger to gently push into the centre and shape each zucotto. Cool before filling.

Piping filling into prunes/dates

Using a piping bag only, pipe filling into prunes/dates, as shown. Piping is far more efficient, and neater, than trying to fill the prunes/dates using a teaspoon. Piping is easy, just practise a little by piping the filling onto baking paper, then re-use it for filling the prunes/dates.

Shaping cornettes

As soon as the baked flat cornettes are cool enough to handle, and before they become crisp, quickly shape and pinch each cornette into a cone shape; hold gently until crisp. Cool on a wire rack.

Rolling licorice

Using a rolling pin (a small one is best, but not essential), roll each strip of soft licorice on baking paper until flattened to about 3mm (⅛ inch) in thickness.

Rolling soft icing

Using rolling pin, gently roll the icings on baking paper or icing-sugared covered surface as evenly as possible, without rolling over the edges, into a flat piece about 3mm (⅛ inch) in thickness. Using a sharp knife, cut the icings into strips, the same length as the licorice.

Stacking soft icing and licorice

Stack the soft icings and the licorice in any coloured layer combination you like.

Cutting bumble-bee licorice

Using sharp knife, cut the stack of licorice and soft icing into bite-sized pieces; place on a baking-paper-covered wire rack to dry. This will take from a few hours to overnight, depending on the weather. Store in an airtight container.

Removing brandy snap from tray

As soon as the snaps are ready to remove from the oven tray, you'll need to work quickly, as they will be beginning to firm and set as they cool. You will work out why we advise to only bake four snaps at the one time. Using a metal spatula, loosen one flat snap from the oven tray.

Shaping brandy snaps

Quickly shape the snap over the bottom of an upturned foil petit four case. If the remaining snaps are too firm to handle, return the tray to the oven for a minute to re-soften; you will become faster at shaping the baskets as you go.

Cutting & layering opera gateau

Cut each cake into a 20cm x 25cm (8-inch x 10-inch) rectangle and a 10cm x 25cm (4-inch x 10-inch) rectangle. Using a pastry brush, brush one of the large rectangles with half the coffee syrup, then spread with half the butter cream. Place the two small rectangles, side-by-side, on top of the butter cream, ensuring all edges and corners are aligned. Brush cakes with the remaining coffee syrup, then spread with the ganache.

Finishing opera gateau

Place the remaining large rectangle on top of ganache, then spread with the remaining buttercream. Refrigerate about 3 hours or until butter cream is firm. Working quickly, spread the glaze evenly over cake, then refrigerate until glaze has set. Glaze must be used while still warm, for a glossy finish to the top of your cake. Use a hot, dry knife to trim any uneven edges before slicing to serve.

Segmenting oranges

Cut a slice off the top and bottom of the orange; stand orange upright and cut all around, just inside pith, to remove peel. Cutting towards the centre, cut down each side of each membrane to form wedges or segments. Segment oranges over a small bowl to catch the juice.

Cooling chocolate hazelnut thins

As soon as the thins are baked, remove them from the oven; quickly slide a metal spatula under each thin to loosen them. Quickly place each warm thin over a rolling pin to cool completely.

Choux pastry

Choux pastry is used to make éclairs, profiteroles (cream puffs) etc. After the butter and water have been brought to the boil, the flour is immediately added to the saucepan, and stirred vigorously (the mixture is quite stiff) over the heat until the ingredients come together and pull away from the side and base of the pan.

More on choux pastry

Transfer the hot mixture to a small high-sided bowl, the beaters need to be right in the mixture. Use an electric mixer to gradually beat in the egg(s), do this on a medium speed. It can be done by hand, but it's hard work. The mixture is ready when all the eggs have been added and the mixture becomes smooth and glossy.

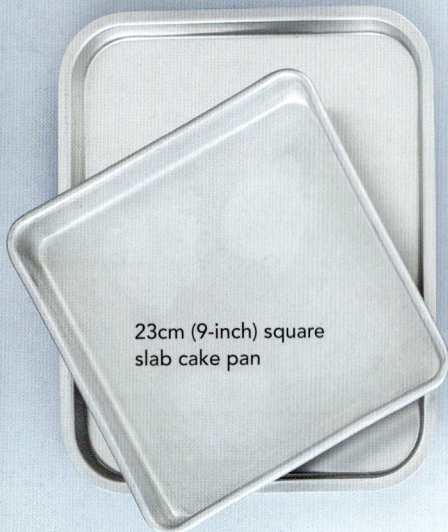

23cm (9-inch) square
slab cake pan

26cm x 30cm swiss roll pan
(10½-inch x 12-inch)

8-hole (¾ cup/180ml) mini loaf pan

12-hole (1½-tablespoon/30ml)
shallow round-based patty pan

6-hole (½ cup/125ml) friand pan

cutters

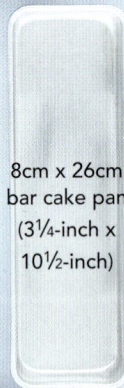

8cm x 26cm
bar cake pan
(3¼-inch x
10½-inch)

19cm x 29cm slice pan
(7¾-inch x 11¾-inch)

6-hole (¾ cup/180ml)
texas muffin pan

9-hole (½ cup/125ml) friand pan

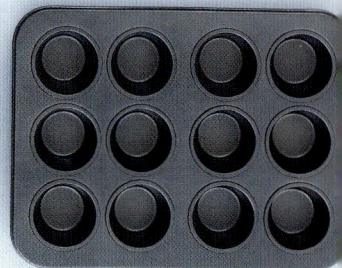

14cm x 21cm loaf pan
(5½-inch x 8½-inch)

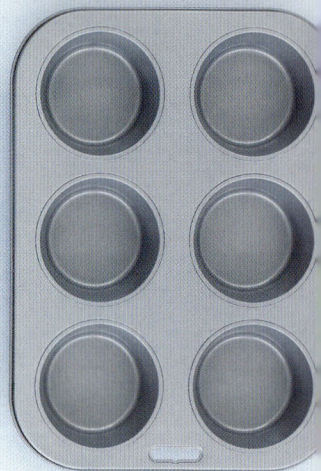

12-hole (1-tablespoon/20ml)
mini muffin pan

equipment

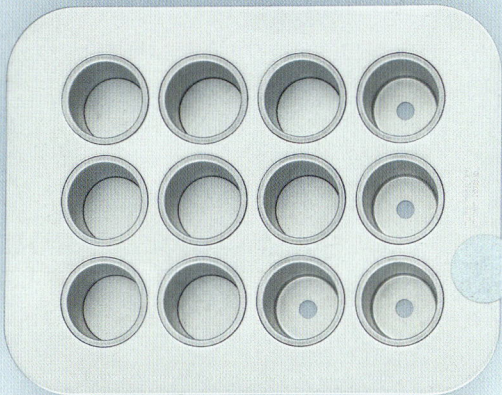

12-hole mini cheesecake pan with removable bases

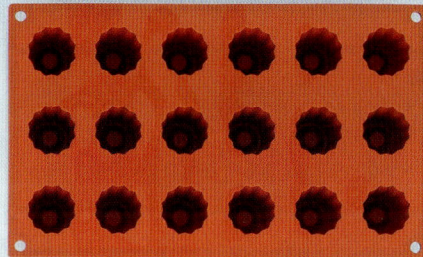

18-hole (1-tablespoon/20ml) flexible jelly mould

15cm x 25cm loaf pan
(6-inch x 10-inch)

6-hole (1-tablespoon/20ml) easter egg mould

12.5cm x 35cm loose-based fluted flan tin (5-inch x 14-inch)

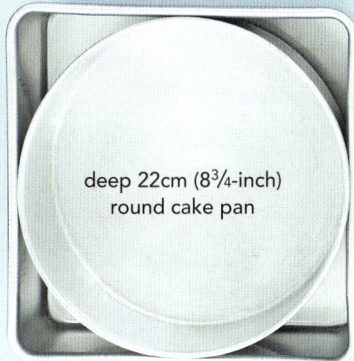

20cm x 30cm lamington pan
(8-inch x 12-inch)

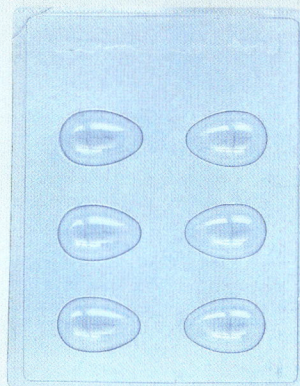

deep 22cm (8¾-inch) round cake pan

deep 23cm (9-inch) square cake pan

10cm (4-inch) round loose-based flan tins

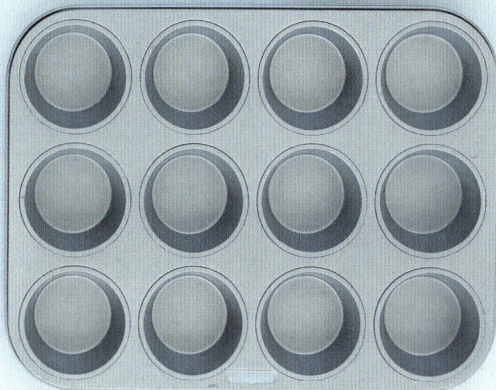

12-hole (⅓ cup/80ml) muffin pan

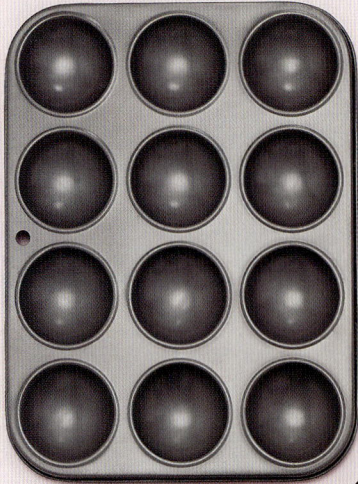

1

2

2

2

2

3

4

5

8

6

7

10

9

11

12

18

19

17

16

16

BakerzBest

30cm
Lightweight

BakerzBest

20cm
Decorating Bag

sales@bakerzbest.com

15

13

14

13

1. round-based patty pans
Available from supermarkets, chain stores and cookware shops, they are also called tartlet pans. They come in a frame of 12, and can be made from aluminium or tin.

2. cutters
Come in all shapes and sizes, and are made from either plastic or metal. Can be bought from specialty cookware shops or cake decorating suppliers.

3. palette knife
The one pictured has a "step", which is good for spreading icings, or there is also the plain bladed (straight) variety. Available from chain stores, supermarkets and cookware shops.

4. pastry brush
Come in handy not only for glazing various foods, but also for cleaning up around cakes.

5. dipping forks
Proper chocolate-dipping forks can be bought from specialty cookware shops, or you can buy the cheap similar versions pictured here, from chain stores.

6. piping tubes
Come in all shapes and sizes, both in metal and plastic; the best quality ones are available from chefs' suppliers and cake decorating suppliers.

7. baking paper
We use baking paper for lining cake pans and making paper piping bags.

8. artist's brush
A few different sized artist's brushes come in handy for things like brushing chocolate inside foil cases.

9. foil cases
These come in a variety of colours and many sizes and thicknesses, from the tiny petit four cases to texas muffin size. Petit four cases are made from a strong, rigid foil. Supermarkets, chain stores and cookware shops carry these cases.

10. colourings
The quality and price of food colourings vary a lot. The more expensive colourings are highly concentrated, so will give more intense colours and will last longer than the more diluted, less expensive colourings.

11. paddle-pop sticks
Used in craft and cooking; we've inserted them in toffee to make a handle for our peanut brittle pops.

12. bamboo skewers
Can be bought from supermarkets and Asian food stores. They come in handy for supporting cakes, as well as testing cakes to see if they are cooked through.

13. paper patty cases
Many coloured, patterned and different-sized cases are available in supermarkets and chain stores, but, if you want specific colours, you'll have to go to cake decorating suppliers.

14. mini muffin pan
Come in a frame consisting of 6, 12 or 24 holes; each hole has a 1-tablespoon capacity. They are available in supermarkets, chain stores and cookware shops.

15. madeleine tin
The traditional French Madeleine cake, for which the tins were designed, is a light mouthful of sponge cake, best eaten fresh from the oven.

16. bought piping bags
Available from supermarkets, cookware shops and chain stores.

17. rolling pin
Come in wood, glass and various synthetic materials; all work well.

18. saucepan with pouring lip
Called milk saucepans; buy the heaviest-based saucepan you can if you're going to use it for making confectionery.

19. candy thermometer
This should be a once-in-a-lifetime investment; keep it in a safe place, away from bumps, preferably wrapped in a tea-towel to protect the bulb from being broken.

glossary

allspice also known as pimento or jamaican pepper; so-named because it tastes like a combination of cumin, nutmeg, clove and cinnamon. Available whole (a dark-brown berry the size of a pea) or ground.

almonds
blanched brown skins removed.
flaked paper-thin slices.
ground also called almond meal.
slivered small pieces cut lengthways.
anise also called aniseed or sweet cumin; the seeds are the fruit of an annual plant native to Greece and Egypt. Dried, they have a strong licorice flavour. Whole and ground seeds are available.

baking paper also called parchment paper or baking parchment; a silicone-coated paper used for lining baking pans and oven trays so cakes and biscuits won't stick.

baking powder a raising agent consisting mainly of two parts cream of tartar to one part bicarbonate of soda (baking soda).

beetroot also known as red beets; firm, round root vegetable.

bicarbonate of soda also known as baking soda.

bottled fruit mince a mix of dried fruits, glacé fruits, nuts, spice, sugar and alcohol; most commonly used to make fruit mince tarts.

butter this book uses salted butter unless stated otherwise; 125g is equal to 1 stick (4 ounces) in other recipes. Unsalted or "sweet" butter has no salt added and is perhaps the most popular among pastry-chefs.

cachous also called dragées in some countries; miniscule (3mm to 5mm) metallic-looking-but-edible confectionery balls used in cake decorating; available in silver, gold or various colours.

cardamom a spice native to India and used extensively in its cuisine; can be purchased in pod, seed or ground form. Has a distinctive aromatic, sweetly rich flavour and is one of the world's most expensive spices. Used to flavour curries, rice dishes, sweet desserts and cakes.

cheese
cream commonly known as philly or philadelphia; a soft, cow-milk cheese.
mascarpone an Italian fresh cultured-cream product made in much the same way as yogurt. Whiteish to creamy yellow in colour, with a buttery-rich, luscious texture. Soft, creamy and spreadable, it is used in many Italian desserts and as an accompaniment to a dessert of fresh fruit.
ricotta soft, sweet, moist, white cow-milk cheese with a low-fat content and a slightly grainy texture.

cherry small, soft stone fruit varying in colour from yellow to dark red. Sweet cherries are eaten whole and in desserts while sour cherries such as the morello variety are used for jams, preserves, pies and savouries.
glacé also called candied cherries; boiled in heavy sugar syrup and then dried. Used in cakes, breads and sweets.

chocolate
Choc Bits also known as chocolate chips or chocolate morsels; available in milk, white and dark chocolate. Made of cocoa liquor, cocoa butter, sugar and an emulsifier, these hold their shape in baking and are ideal for decorating.
couverture a term used to describe a fine quality, very rich chocolate high in both cocoa butter and cocoa liquor. Requires tempering when used to coat but not if used in baking, mousses or fillings.
dark cooking also called compounded chocolate; good for cooking as it doesn't require tempering and sets at room temperature. Made with vegetable fat instead of cocoa butter so it lacks the rich, buttery flavour of eating chocolate. Cocoa butter is the most expensive component in chocolate, so the substitution of a vegetable fat means that compounded chocolate is much cheaper to produce.

dark eating also known as semi-sweet or luxury chocolate; made of a high percentage of cocoa liquor and cocoa butter, and little added sugar. Unless stated otherwise, we use dark eating chocolate in this book as it's ideal for use in desserts and cakes.

Melts small discs of compounded milk, white or dark chocolate ideal for melting and moulding.

milk eating most popular eating chocolate; mild and very sweet.

white eating contains no cocoa solids but derives its sweet flavour from cocoa butter. Very sensitive to heat.

chocolate hazelnut spread also known as Nutella.

cinnamon available in pieces (called sticks or quills) and ground. The dried inner bark of the shoots of the Sri Lankan native cinnamon tree.

cloves can be used whole or in ground form. Has a strong scent and taste, so should be used minimally.

coco pops are chocolate-flavoured rice bubbles.

cocoa powder also called cocoa; unsweetened, dried, roasted then ground cocoa beans.

coconut

desiccated unsweetened, dried, concentrated, shredded coconut.

flaked dried flaked coconut flesh.

shredded unsweetened thin strips of dried coconut flesh.

corn syrup an imported product available in some supermarkets, delicatessens and health food stores. Made from cornstarch, it is a popular ingredient in American cooking for frostings, jams and jellies.

cornflakes commercially made cereal; dehydrated then baked crisp flakes of corn.

cornflour also known as cornstarch. Available made from corn or wheat (wheaten cornflour, gluten-free, gives a lighter texture in cakes); used as a thickening agent in cooking.

cream

double very rich, versatile cream; it withstands boiling, and whips and freezes well.

pouring also called pure cream. It has no additives and contains a minimum fat content of 35 per cent. If a recipe here calls for an unspecified cream, this is the one we use.

sour cream a thick, commercially-cultured sour cream with a minimum fat content of 35 per cent.

thickened a whipping cream that contains a thickener. It has a minimum fat content of 35 per cent.

cream of tartar the acid ingredient in baking powder; when added to confectionery mixtures it helps to prevent sugar crystallising.

crème fraîche a naturally fermented cream having a velvety texture and slightly tangy, nutty flavour.

custard powder instant mixture used to make pouring custard; similar to North American instant pudding mixes.

dried cranberries also called craisins; available from the dried fruit section in most supermarkets.

eggs we use large chicken eggs having an average weight of 60g unless stated otherwise. If recipes call for raw or barely cooked eggs, exercise caution if there is a salmonella problem in your area, particularly for children and pregnant women.

essence synthetically produced substances used in small amounts to impart their flavours to foods.

figs originally from the countries that border the eastern Mediterranean; are best eaten in peak season, at the height of summer. Figs are also glacéd (candied), dried or canned in sugar syrup; usually sold at health-food stores, Middle Eastern food shops or specialty cheese counters.

flour

plain also called all-purpose; made from wheat flour, it is the best for baking: the gluten content ensures a strong dough, which produces a light result.

rice very fine, gluten-free flour; made from ground white rice.

self-raising all-purpose plain flour with baking powder added in the proportion of 1 cup flour to 2 teaspoons baking powder.

wholemeal also called wholewheat flour; milled with the wheat germ so is higher in fibre and more nutritional than plain flour.

food colouring vegetable-based substances; available in liquid, paste or gel form.

gelatine a thickening agent. We use powdered gelatine; is also available in sheets called leaf gelatine.

ginger

glacé fresh ginger root preserved in sugar syrup; crystallised ginger can be substituted if rinsed with warm water and dried before using.

ground also known as powdered ginger; used as a flavouring in cakes, pies and puddings but cannot be substituted for fresh ginger.

glacé fruit fruit such as pineapple, apricots, peaches and pears cooked in a heavy syrup and then dried.

glucose syrup also known as liquid glucose; made from wheat starch.

gold leaf (edible) available from cake decorating or art supply stores.

golden syrup a by-product of refined sugarcane; pure maple syrup or honey can often be substituted.

hazelnuts also known as filberts; plump, grape-size, rich, sweet nut having a brown inedible skin that is removed by rubbing heated nuts together vigorously in a tea-towel.

ground also called hazelnut meal; is made by grounding the hazelnuts to a coarse floury texture and is used in baking or as a thickening agent.

honey the variety sold in a squeezable container is not suitable for the recipes in this book.

ice-cream we use a good quality ice-cream having 5g of fat per 100ml for the recipes in this book.

liqueur

cherry-flavoured use Kirsch or any generic brand.

coconut-flavoured use Malibu or any generic brand.

coffee-flavoured use Tia Maria, Kahlua or any generic brand.

hazelnut-flavoured use Frangelico or any generic brand.

mint-flavoured use Crème de Menthe or any generic brand.

orange-flavoured use Cointreau, Grand Marnier or any generic brand.

macadamias native to Australia; fairly large, slightly soft, buttery rich nut. Should always be stored in the fridge to prevent their high oil content turning them rancid.

maple-flavoured syrup is made from sugar cane and is also known

as golden or pancake syrup. It is not a substitute for pure maple syrup.

maple syrup distilled from the sap of maple trees found only in Canada and parts of North America. Maple-flavoured syrup or pancake syrup is not an adequate substitute for the real thing.

marzipan also called almond paste; a paste made from ground almonds, sugar and water.

milk we use full-cream homogenised milk unless otherwise specified.

buttermilk originally the term given to the slightly sour liquid left after butter was churned from cream, today it is made similarly to yogurt. Sold alongside all fresh milk products in supermarkets. Despite the implication of its name, it is low in fat.

evaporated unsweetened canned milk from which water has been extracted by evaporation.

full-cream powder instant powdered milk made from whole cow milk with the liquid removed and emulsifiers added.

sweetened condensed a canned milk product consisting of milk with more than half the water content removed and sugar added to the remaining milk.

top 'n' fill caramel a canned milk product made of condensed milk that has been boiled to a caramel.

mixed fruit a combination of sultanas, raisins, currants, mixed peel and cherries.

mixed peel candied citrus peel.

mixed spice a classic mixture generally containing caraway, allspice, coriander, cumin, nutmeg and ginger, although cinnamon and other spices can be added.

molasses a thick, dark brown syrup, the residue from the refining of sugar; available in light, dark and blackstrap varieties. It is slightly bitter in taste.

nutmeg a strong and pungent spice ground from the dried nut of an evergreen tree native to Indonesia. Usually found ground but the flavour is more intense from a whole nut, available from spice shops, so it's best to grate your own. Found in mixed spice mixtures.

orange blossom water distilled from orange blossoms.

peanut butter a creamy blend of ground peanuts, vegetable oil and salt. Available smooth or crunchy.

peanuts also called groundnut, not in fact a nut but the pod of a legume.

pecans native to the US and now grown locally; pecans are golden brown, buttery and rich. Good in savoury as well as sweet dishes; walnuts are a good substitute.

peppermint oil from the peppermint plant; often used as a flavouring.

pistachios green, delicately flavoured nuts inside hard off-white shells. Available salted or unsalted in their shells; you can also get them shelled.

plain sweet biscuits crisp, sweet, vanilla flavoured biscuits.

popcorn a variety of corn that is sold as kernels for popping corn, or can be bought ready-popped.

quince paste available from most supermarkets and delicatessens.

ready-rolled pastry packaged sheets of frozen shortcrust, butter puff, or puff pastry; available from supermarkets.

rhubarb a plant with long, green-red stalks; becomes sweet and edible when cooked.

rolled oats flattened oat grain rolled into flakes and traditionally used for porridge. Instant oats are also available, but use traditional oats for baking.

rosewater extract made from crushed rose petals.

soft icing also known as prepared fondant and ready-to-roll icing.

sugar we use coarse, granulated table sugar, also known as crystal sugar, unless otherwise specified.

brown a very soft, finely granulated sugar retaining molasses for its characteristic colour and flavour.

caster also known as superfine or finely granulated table sugar.

demerara small-grained golden-coloured crystal sugar.

icing also called confectioners' sugar or powdered sugar; pulverised granulated sugar crushed together with a small amount (about 3 per cent) of cornflour.

pure icing also called confectioners' sugar or powdered sugar, and does not contain cornflour.

raw natural brown granulated sugar.

white a coarse, granulated table sugar, also known as crystal sugar.

vanilla

bean dried, long, thin pod from a tropical golden orchid grown in central and South America and Tahiti; the minuscule black seeds inside the bean are used to impart a luscious vanilla flavour. Place a whole bean in a jar of sugar to make the vanilla sugar often called for in recipes; a bean can be used three or four times before losing its flavour.

extract obtained from vanilla beans infused in water; a non-alcoholic version of essence.

vegetable oil any of a number of oils sourced from plant rather than animal fats.

vinegar

malt brown-coloured vinegar made from fermented malt and beech shavings.

white made from distilled grain alcohol.

conversion chart

measures

One Australian metric measuring cup holds about 250ml; one Australian metric tablespoon holds 20ml; one Australian metric teaspoon holds 5ml. The difference between one country's measuring cups and another's is within a two- or three-teaspoon variance, and will not affect your cooking results. North America, New Zealand and the United Kingdom use a 15ml tablespoon.

All cup and spoon measurements are level. The most accurate way of measuring dry ingredients is to weigh them. When measuring liquids, use a clear glass or plastic jug with the metric markings.

We use large eggs with an average weight of 60g.

The imperial measurements used in these recipes are approximate only.

oven temperatures

The oven temperatures in this book are for conventional ovens; if you have a fan-forced oven, decrease the temperature by 10-20 degrees.

	°C (CELSIUS)	°F (FAHRENHEIT)
Very slow	120	250
Slow	150	300
Moderately slow	160	325
Moderate	180	350
Moderately hot	200	400
Hot	220	425
Very hot	240	475

dry measures

METRIC	IMPERIAL
15g	½oz
30g	1oz
60g	2oz
90g	3oz
125g	4oz (¼lb)
155g	5oz
185g	6oz
220g	7oz
250g	8oz (½lb)
280g	9oz
315g	10oz
345g	11oz
375g	12oz (¾lb)
410g	13oz
440g	14oz
470g	15oz
500g	16oz (1lb)
750g	24oz (1½lb)
1kg	32oz (2lb)

liquid measures

METRIC	IMPERIAL
30ml	1 fluid oz
60ml	2 fluid oz
100ml	3 fluid oz
125ml	4 fluid oz
150ml	5 fluid oz (¼ pint/1 gill)
190ml	6 fluid oz
250ml	8 fluid oz
300ml	10 fluid oz (½ pint)
500ml	16 fluid oz
600ml	20 fluid oz (1 pint)
1000ml (1 litre)	1¾ pints

length measures

METRIC	IMPERIAL
3mm	⅛in
6mm	¼in
1cm	½in
2cm	¾in
2.5cm	1in
5cm	2in
6cm	2½in
8cm	3in
10cm	4in
13cm	5in
15cm	6in
18cm	7in
20cm	8in
23cm	9in
25cm	10in
28cm	11in
30cm	12in (1ft)

index